MW01200317

AFTER NINE HUNDRED YEARS

Divided Christendom: A Catholic Study of the Problem of Reunion, 1939

Christ, Our Lady and the Church, 1957

Lay People in the Church, 1957

AFTER NINE HUNDRED YEARS

THE BACKGROUND OF THE SCHISM BETWEEN THE EASTERN AND WESTERN CHURCHES

YVES CONGAR, O.P.

FORDHAM UNIVERSITY PRESS

NEW YORK

Library of Congress Cataloging in Publication Data

Congar, Yves Marie Joseph, 1904-
   After nine hundred years.

   Translation of Neuf cents ans après, originally
published as v. 1, pt. 1 of L'Eglise et les églises,
1054-1954.

   Bibliography: p.
   Includes index.
   1. Schism--Eastern and Western Church. I. Title.
BX303.C613   270.3'8
  ISBN 0-8232-1857-0   LC 59-15643

© 1959 Fordham University Press

A Translation of Neuf cents ans après, originally published
as part of 1054-1954, L'Eglise et Les Eglises Editions de
Chevetogne, Belgium

ISBN 0-8232-1857-0

LC 59-15643

Printed in the United States of America

10 9 8 7 6 5 4

TABLE OF CONTENTS

PREFACE

On January 25, 1959, His Holiness Pope John XXIII, still in the opening months of his pontificate, made known to the world his intention of convoking an Ecumenical Council which would be "an invitation to the separated Christian Communities to find unity."

It seemed to us that it would be an excellent preparation for the reconciliation of Eastern and Western Christians, if we were to assist in making available in an English translation the masterly study of Father Yves Congar, O.P., first published in 1954. We were fortunate in receiving the enthusiastic approval of Father Congar for the project and he has been kind enough to supplement his original text with considerable new material and to bring up to date the already abundant bibliography and copious notes of the first edition.

The year 1954 marked the ninth centenary of the excommunication pronounced by the legates of the Holy See against Michael Cerularius, Patriarch of Constantinople, a date which for long has been accepted as that of the break between Rome and Byzantium. As a result of his long and profound studies of the relations of East and West from the earliest days of Christianity, Father Congar has seen, and exposes with luminous clarity, the many political, cultural, and ecclesiological influences which have tended, long before 1054, to bring about an estrangement between the Oriental and the Western Churches. Even after that memorable date, he shows us the numerous occasions when a lack of mutual understanding, resulting from deeply-rooted psychological prejudices, closed men's minds and, unfortunately, caused serious breaches of charity. Ignorance and disdain lasting for centuries, inevitably brought it about that each went its own way, oblivious and unaware of the other.

It is in *the acceptance of this estrangement* that Father Congar finds the real Oriental Schism. Separation was growing in the minds and hearts of men before it took place in the pages of History. If, under the guidance of the Holy Spirit, a reconciliation is to take place, it will surely begin and grow under the warming rays of Divine Charity and men will learn to understand, to respect and to love one another, each for what they are.

Through the collaboration of the staff of Fordham University Press and that of the Russian Center of Fordham University, the original work, which in French is so rich and suggestive in the conciseness of its thought, has been carefully translated into English.

Paul Mailleux, S.J.

*Graeci, qui nobiscum sunt
et nobiscum non sunt,
juncti fide, pace divisi.*

St. Bernard of Clairvaux
De Consideratione, III.1.

Figures in the text refer to
notes beginning on page 91.

CHAPTER ONE

THE CENTURIES-OLD ESTRANGEMENT OF THE EASTERN AND WESTERN CHURCHES

The year 1054 is indeed a memorable date in the history of the Church. However, this date is more a symbolic than an historical one, such as are the dates of October 31, 1517, or July 14, 1789, from which we are accustomed to date "the beginning of the Reformation," or "the beginning of the French Revolution," respectively. The following pages will once again illustrate the thesis, rather generally acccepted today,[1] that July, 1054, cannot be put down as marking the beginning of the "Oriental Schism." These pages do not pretend to bring any new information to the historian familiar with the events called to mind: he will more likely be inclined to correct and complete what is but a rough sketch revealing the limitations of the non-specialist. Only a certain number of facts and significant references have been marshalled here for the purpose of suggesting to theologians and churchmen some thoughts on the nature of the "Oriental schism." If our rough outline is accurate, those two words can with justification be placed within quotation marks.

Not that the words do not express something very real: historically, canonically and theologically, the Oriental schism, unfortunately, is a fact. It can be defined according to the canonical and doctrinal criteria of the Catholic Church, criteria which, needless to say, we accept unequivocally. Those criteria are simple: they may be summed up as the union with the Apostolic See of Rome on the basis of a recognition of its primacy as coming from Christ and the Apostles. In the light of these, we can determine quite accurately when and where schism has occurred. The separation may likewise be attributed to any one of the local churches with the exception of the Church of Rome, for she, while being also a local church, is something else too: as a local church which belongs to the union of the Universal Church, she has an autonomous and decisive value. Legitimate authority can act wrongly: yet one may not separate oneself from it and the final wrong lies always on the side of those who cause separation.

When a dispute concerns a church or an ensemble of churches and not merely an individual or individuals, when what is at stake is an historical situation which involves the complex reality of collective rather than individual responsibility,[2] the problem becomes far more complicated. We would speak of the schism of Photius, the schism of Cerularius, and many others without the use of quotation marks; not so with the "Oriental schism." The latter cannot be put in the same category with the former: it presents an original problem with elements and values involving other considerations, the most important of which we shall try to suggest in the following pages.

That this is so, is borne out by the fact that the break-up had begun before Photius and Cerularius, that it was not completed after the latter's time and was not concluded all at once, or even in a consistent manner, in the various Eastern

2

churches. To present it as a declaration of war to which a date can be assigned, or as a state of hostility inaugurated by a single and definable act—even though followed by temporary but complete and satisfactory reconciliations—would be a fiction to which the facts do not correspond. As has often been said before, there were numerous breaches between Rome and Constantinople or another portion of the East, before Michael Cerularius and even before Photius himself.[3] According to Marxist dictum, quantity, carried to a certain degree, modifies the category and becomes quality. One cannot consider 217 years of separation in 506 years of history without realizing that this does not mean normal union simply interrupted by accidents. On the other hand, the instances of union are so numerous between the year 1054 and the Council of Florence, that it is even less correct to speak of total separation merely punctuated by some happy accidents, or by exceptions. Many instances of union still existed[4] even after the rejection of the Council of Florence by the Eastern churches—a date which, were it absolutely necessary to indicate a beginning, would be the best chronological reference mark for the true beginning of the schism;[5] moreover, union was not rejected at once and immediately everywhere.[6] This time, however, the instances of union were sufficiently exceptional to warrant speaking of them as fortuitous happenings. The fact remains that this "Oriental schism" which began before Cerularius, was not completed with him and, in a sense, never has been totally carried through.

There were many differences and many inconsistencies existing from place to place. Very often, local churches broke the union with other churches, or even with Rome; sometimes, however, they maintained union among themselves and with Rome, while they either remained in communion with, or broke away from, various churches that had different relations among one another. The indivisible character of the communion is an old ecclesiological principle, sanctioned by a canon of the first Ecumenical Council (Nicaea, Can. 5), but it is far from having always been applied.[7] From this viewpoint as well, the "Oriental schism" cannot be dealt with as a homogeneous, and if I may say so, monolithic, entity.

An essential fact emerges from all this: the "Oriental schism" extends over a long period of history; in many respects it is coextensive with the very history of the Church, at least since the Fourth Century and even before. It is in this framework and according to these dimensions that the "Oriental schism" must be interpreted, not only when recounting its history, but even when attempting to give a theological interpretation of it. The theological *analysis* of the notion of schism can be considered to have been made and rather well; but a further task must be undertaken, namely, the theological *interpretation* of the great facts of history, of concrete situations such as the one under discussion—the "Oriental schism"— and the situation in which the Roman Catholic Church, and the Oriental Church separated from Rome, find themselves in relation to each other and in relation to the unity to be promoted.

If nothing more than the analysis of the notion of schism were involved, the task would be relatively simple and easy. It would suffice to define the sin of schism and the unity which it destroys. But when one passes from the sin of schism personally and formally committed, to Christian com-

4

munities in a state of schism, the thing becomes rather more complicated. In this connection, Monsignor Journet has made a new aṅd extremely interesting study,[8] which remains, however, on the plane of a theological presentation of typical cases or typical circumstances. Would it not be desirable to extend the effort to a *theological interpretation* of history itself, of the *historical reality* implied by the words "Oriental schism?" While in the theology of schism *per se*, the one who breaks away is absolutely in the wrong, here the wrongs are not all on one side, as Humbert of Romans remarked long ago.[9]

The aim of these pages is to suggest to theologians a few elements of an interpretation of the historical reality of the "Oriental schism." Briefly, the "schism" appears to us as the acceptance of a situation by which each part of Christendom lives, behaves and judges without taking notice one of the other. We may call it geographical remoteness, provincialism, lack of contact, a "state of reciprocal ignorance,"[10] alienation,[11] or by the German word "Entfremdung."[12] The English word "estrangement" expresses all this quite admirably. The Oriental schism came about by a progressive estrangement: this is the conclusion to which the following analysis seems to lead us.

For several reasons we have restricted the extent of our treatment in this book: first, by omitting developments which would have necessitated a more thorough elaboration of many questions; secondly, to show that the present account does not pretend to be exhaustive; third, and principally, to indicate the tentative, quasi-hypothetical character of our remarks: what we have to say is really in the realm of basic research. We thus consciously accept the risk of being reproached for schematization, when we frankly merely list the various aspects, causes, or manifestations of the global and continuous fact of this estrangement, and likewise give unequal development to the different respective sections which we sometimes limit to simple notations, even when they deal with quite important points. We shall begin by examining the outward—the historical—framework, and then proceed to the core of the question by examining, in this order, the political, the cultural, and the ecclesiological factors.

CHAPTER TWO

POLITICAL FACTORS CONTRIBUTING TO THE ESTRANGEMENT

THE LEGACY OF THE NEW ROME CREATED BY CONSTAN-
TINE AND THE BURDEN OF A CHURCH OF THE EMPIRE.

The division of the Roman Empire into two parts was
perhaps inevitable for there had already been the Tetrarchy of
Diocletian in 292. However, the split that is here under
study, the seed of which was indisputably planted by Constantine, finally had an effect on the Church itself. For this
reason it is important that we understand the cause and the
consequences of this act of Constantine, of creating a new
capital in Byzantium.

The cause is not to be found merely in the fact of a new
capital in Byzantium, in the early years of the Fourth Century,
but in the vast complex of ideas and practices which linked
the essential realities of the Empire with the essential realities
of the Church: an identification of the center of the Church
with the center of the Empire, a joining of the highest ecclesiastical reality of the Church to the highest civil reality
of the Empire, which united the whole life of the Church to
the Emperor and to his authority. It was a concept of a
Church within the framework of the Empire, to become
as it were, *the Church of the Empire*, much more than a mere

parallel existence of the two powers, or, as they would say in the East, a "symphony."[1] Such is the Christian interpretation, according to which the best men of the Church, especially the popes, try to line up the facts. Such has been, and still is, the Christian ideal. But Constantine achieved something else and he has transmitted it through many centuries to the Christian world, something else and more. It consists of some very extensive elements of the pagan system giving the Emperor the quality of Sovereign in religious matters as well as in civil affairs. The separation of powers was unknown in antiquity, but it became an acquisition characteristic of the Middle Ages, especially in the West, through the action of the papacy. The intentions of Constantine are not in question: the Oriental Church canonized him; there can be absolutely no doubt about his religious sincerity and his Christian faith. But it still is the old pagan system which became Christian only in the person of the Emperor, and which was transferred in large part to the shores of the Bosphorus. The thesis of Am. Gasquet needs to be rewritten in the light of new knowledge about Byzantium which indeed we have only recently acquired.[2] But the general lines of Gasquet's thesis remain solid and are corroborated by the studies of others.[3]

The quasi-sacerdotal role of the Emperor and its effect on the theological concept of a universal church.

According to this system, the Emperor had a sovereign role in the matter of worship. Not that he celebrated the mysteries and preached the word of God as do priests—although the Byzantine *Basileis* often delivered veritable sermons and intervened in dogmatic questions—[4]: his situation was more to be compared to that of Elizabeth of England according to the 37th of the XXXIX Articles, but the person of the *Basileus* was more sacred, had a quasi-sacerdotal, almost episcopal character.[5] The charge of the Emperor, his sovereignty, was simultaneously exercised in matters of religion and was therefore ecclesiastical, but kept itself within the bounds of *coercive power*. It was, in effect, the power of the State. But instead of confining itself to the temporal order, this power existed and was exercised in the domain of the Church. It is well known that the Emperor appointed the patriarchs of Constantinople, created or modified the ecclesiastical districts and the episcopal Sees, convoked Councils, supervised the proceedings of their deliberations, declared them closed, and above all *gave the value of Imperial law to their decisions*—in our opinion the essential point. Thus, for the organization of the Ecumenical Church ("Ecumenical"—"of the Empire")[6] and for the regulation of her life, the Emperor exercised his authority conjointly with the bishops.[7] Seen in this perspective, there was the danger that the *juridical* attributes of the Church, the aspect of authority and coercion that she bears as a society would, in an Established Church, make these attributes practically Imperial, and not Apostolic. It could perhaps be debated whether such an interpretation of the famous declaration of Constantine, "Bishop from without,"[8] should be accepted; however, we should be inclined to do so for what there is of real historical meaning in the episode rather than for the literal meaning of the words.

When the Patriarch Nil wrote in an act of 1380: "The authority of the *Basileus* regulates by law exterior and visible things, while the Church is experienced in the things within, the things of the soul (of the νοῦς)"[9] he was giving a theological formula of the situation created by Constantine. But one may hesitate over the ecclesiological implications of both Constantine's invention and the Patriarch's formula. In *Divided Christendom*, we have advanced the idea that the Byzantine ecclesiology had, through Constantine, an entirely mystical idea of the Church, and refused to develop its juridical aspects.[10] The question is certainly more intricate than that, and it involves a whole complex of thought. Moreover, as V. Lossky has rightly remarked, we must not forget "the stupendous wealth of canonical tradition of the Orthodox Church,"[11] aside from the properly theological treatises. Perhaps, even so, a certain incapability of perceiving how the "visible" and "exterior" are themselves of the Church—an inability particularly felt in the Slavophile systematization[12]—has its origins in the sequence of events that we shall try to retrace.

At this point also we cannot refrain from mentioning the thesis of Jalland.[13] This writer has placed the question of the papacy and the Roman primacy in the framework of the problems posed by the need for unity—unity for the Empire, to begin with, then and above all, unity for the Church. The Empire, before Diocletian, was more or less a federation of cities and provinces. Diocletian organized it, dividing it into two great administrative domains, and promoted political unity: the cult of the Emperor which the Christian refused, thereby provoking a very serious persecution, was a means toward unity. It is into this same perspective of a policy of unity for the Empire that the actions of Constantine may be fitted, along with the legislation that stemmed from the "Edict of Milan." Thenceforth, and thanks to the role played by the Emperor in the Church, the unity of the

Empire was sought within the Christian framework, taking account of the delays permitted and the circumspection observed in regard to a mortally-wounded paganism. This entire evolution, thinks Jalland, continued to present a grave problem for the Church. In an Empire that was provincial, the Church had existed as something of a federation—more exactly, a fraternity or a union—of local churches; such a semi-clandestine regime adapted itself rather well to the situation. But in a unified Empire, especially a unified Empire that had become Christian in the person of the Emperor, the Church, from then on part of the ecumenical life of the Empire, found it necessary to elaborate her ecumenical organization and her theory of ecumenical authority. A great many happenings of the Fourth and Fifth Centuries become clear, as Jalland shows,[14] if we interpret them in the light of this question: "Will the ecumenical authority in the Church be the Apostolic institution and tradition, or will it be the *dogma* of the Emperor?"

The persistent theme of the Popes' opposition to the *Basileus* and the Patriarch of Constantinople was their refusal to accept the idea that any exercise of juridical power on the part of the Church in the Empire derived from some political or imperial statute. They insisted, in these cases, that it flowed from an Apostolic law, one properly ecclesiastical, particularly in the case of supreme authority in the Universal Church, which it is the divine prerogative of Rome to exercise. The crisis, a veritably endemic one after Nicaea, was to become decidedly acute when Rome, politically emancipated from the Empire, could more independently assert the right to regulate the canonical life of the Universal Church without appeal. In this respect, all the events which were to render the Church more effectively independent of Constantinople and the *Basileus* were to have their ecclesiological and canonical repercussions. Among these events were: the conversion of the barbarian kings and peoples upon whom the Church depended in the West (a fact that was resented in Constantinople, as was clearly noticeable at the end of the Sixth Century); the emergence of Pepin the Short and Charlemagne; the *Donatio Constantini*, to which we will refer later on; and the establishment of the Normans in the southern part of Italy to the direct injury of Constantinople, a step which provided the context for the affair of Michael Cerularius.

Thus the relations between Rome and Constantinople have often represented so many occasions for a struggle and a competition wherein the point at issue sometimes had juridico-political aspects (Illyricum, the Bulgars), but was fundamentally an ecclesiological concept. Rome followed the logic of a Universal Church centered round its primacy. In this, she obeyed her profound vocation, based on the institution of Our Lord and on the presence of the Apostles Peter and Paul; she was likewise favored by various factors that were both political and natural: the Roman genius, the ideological and sentimental heritage of Imperial Rome, and the fact, which Baumstark[15] stresses, that in a West occupied by the barbarians Rome appeared as a center and even as a unique source of civilization. She had complete freedom to realize, in the peoples who did not erect against her the barriers of a secular culture and a Christianity that already had its own existence, a life of a unified Church, which was Latin and, finally, Roman. These and other data which reveal the social and ecclesiological history of the West, provided the ecclesiology of the Universal Church with every chance to take hold in that part of Christianity. This ecclesiology, however, ran the grave risk of being seriously tinged with Latinism and juridicism.

In the East, on the contrary, Christianity developed from the beginning in various regional and very ancient cultures. There, according to the extent that Constantinople dominated (and this extent varied according to political destinies), it was the idea of a Church of Empire, ecumenical in that sense, which prevailed, with the ecclesiological risks pointed out above.[16] The rise of the authority of the Ecumenical Patriarch (authority *de facto* stronger than authority *de jure*), even in the times, (more numerous than is often thought) when this authority displayed an independence towards the *Basileus*, took place within the framework of the Imperial idea. Moreover, while the existence of local churches, with their own liturgical language and their autonomy, had from the beginning oriented people's minds towards the idea of a communion or fraternity of churches, the aggressive contact with Islam made Byzantium consolidate herself as a nation confronting other national powers, and the Byzantine Church thus became a national Greek Church.[17] The idea of an organization of the Church on a universal plane, with an appropriate hierarchical court of appeal, had not the least chance of finding favor in Eastern thought. Baumstark notes with subtlety[18] that the West approaches ecclesiastical reality in an analytical way; to begin with, the *whole* is posited, then the particular communions are conceived of as parts of this whole. In the East what is first envisaged are the local churches, then the exigencies of their communion are postulated. In the West, one prays for the unity of the Church ("pro

Ecclesia tua sancta catholica, quam pacificare, custodire, adunare et regere digneris toto orbe terrarum, una cum famulo tuo papa nostro..."; "ne respicias peccata mea, sed fidem Ecclesiae tuae..."); in the East, one prays "for the prosperity of the holy Churches of God."[19] In the West, the first and concrete given fact is the total unity, in the East, it is the local diversity. In the West, separation is all the more felt as a scandal, a kind of amputation which mutilates the body; in the East, unity is regarded more as an ideal, as a family reunion can be a reunion in which many things can, at one time or another, prevent one or the other member from taking part. In fact, among the Eastern Churches it is impossible not to be struck by a certain lack of any uneasiness or discomfort in the midst of multiple and often, rather long interruptions of communion.[20]

For all these reasons and still others, the ecclesiological acquisitions of the West (an ecclesiology of the universal Church and a hierarchical court of appeal, likewise universal and apostolic in origin) have remained foreign to the East. On the other hand, the ecclesiological significance of the local Church, centered on the mystery and the sacrament, which has unceasingly inspired Eastern thought, has played a smaller part in this half of Christendom.

The pagan concept of the Roman Empire and the Byzantine ideal of the Emperor as God's representative.

The position taken by Constantinople in regard to Rome was largely fostered by the powerful Roman ideology that had been transferred to Constantinople, the 'New Rome.' The politico-religious thought of the Emperors and the people was to be affected first; the canonico-theological thought of the Patriarchs and clergy was to be affected later.

The idea of Constantinople as the New Rome was not that of Constantine himself, but it devolved from his action, and the transference of all the τάξις of ancient Rome to Byzantium. The theme has been treated in many publications.[21] Along with the immense prestige of Rome, there was in Byzantium the consciousness of continuing the Roman Empire; this, too, has often been emphasized by the commentators;[22] (Ῥωμαῖος = Byzantine).[23] It was inevitable, especially in the actual and ideological framework of a Church of Empire, that the idea of Constantinople as New Rome should entail ecclesiological and canonical consequences, the very ones that are generally and quite simply classed under the heading "ambition of the Patriarchs of Constantinople." We will return to this later in our comments. If there had been a transfer of Empire, it was reasoned, there had consequently also been a transfer of ecclesiological primacy.[24]

Needless to say, Rome regarded with coolness, or rather affected to ignore, the idea of Constantinople as a New Rome.[25] Likewise, from the Eighth Century onward, in order to hold back the spread of this idea, Rome made use of the famous *Donatio Constantini*, one of the most harmful pieces of forgery known to history (and not merely to the history of Rome).[26] It was a weapon, moreover, which betrayed the very cause of Rome, since by argument *ad hominem*, the *Donatio* in seeking to check an Emperor, presents the dignity of Peter and his successors and the privileges attached to that position as emanating from the political power of an Emperor and not from the Apostolic institution.[27] Byzantium retained all the more the logic of her positions by retorting with her own argument from the Tenth Century onward, and by relying upon the *Donatio* to affirm that Constantine had transferred all the τάξις to Constantinople, including that of making decisions in ecclesiastical affairs.[28]

The transfer of the ideology of Rome to Byzantium constituted for the East and for a Church of Empire a principle all the more powerful in that it was reinforced by what we may call the "unitarian" ideal or idea. According to this idea, terrestrial government and the terrestrial order of things imitate celestial government and the celestial order of things; therefore, there can be on earth but one order, one truth, one justice, one power, of which the custodian is the image and representative of God; to *one* God in Heaven, *one* sole monarch corresponds on earth, by right at least. The origins of these ideas have been traced[29] from Aristotle (whether in the original text which ends the *Metaphysics* or in the "plato nizing" text found in *De Mundo*), passing through Philo Judaeus down to Eusebius of Caesarea, the thinker who has expressed the idea most theologically by applying it precisely to the Christian Empire of Constantine. Despite his weakness in theology, the influence of Eusebius cannot be exaggerated.[30] Christian society is in the image of the Heavenly Kingdom, and of the *politeia* of Heaven. It embraces in a unique order, under the authority of the Emperor, all the aspects of life. By right, it covers the whole world and thus the Byzantine *Basileis* affirmed their right to the obedience of the barbarian and pagan kings themselves, beyond the frontiers of the Empire.

This "unitarian" ideology reigned in Byzantium.[31] Indeed, a thesis could be developed on the idea of sovereignty which resulted from it. It also prevailed in the West, at least from the Eighth Century onward, first of all to the profit of the Emperor (from Charlemagne to Gregory VII), then rather to the profit of the Pope—not without claims asserted on the part of the temporal monarchs. A great many things in the history of Christianity may be explained if one keeps this "unitarian idea" in mind. The instances are almost innumerable. Here we need interest ourselves in these themes only from the viewpoint of the estrangement, which we will try to understand in its origin and development. It might not go beyond the facts to state that in Byzantium there prevailed the idea of a transfer of the universal sovereignty of God to a "unitarian" order; but this transfer was more imperial than ecclesiastical. The idea that the unity of the Kingdom should be reflected in the *Church*, in its very structure, was not applied as far as the visible and social features of the Church were concerned, but it remained entirely mystical in the order of prayer and sacraments.[32]

Besides, considering the total Christian world, there was not merely one "unitarian" order but two: therefore, one too many. For opposing the Byzantine *Basileus* there arose another "Emperor." And, opposing the Emperor and finally confronting any monarch claiming to be the sovereign head of the Christian world, the pope raised a higher claim, progressively expressed in occasional assertions of power, first in Canon law—in the Eighth to Eleventh Century—then in theology—in the Thirteenth Century—and finally in dogma, by the Vatican Council.

Rome under barbarian rulers: treason of the ideal

But many episodes in the history of Western Christianity have completely betrayed the Byzantine ideal just defined.

We generally blame both sides in this betrayal; it has also been said that the *Basileis* lacked a feeling of solidarity with the West which they abandoned to its destiny save for a few attempts such as the grandiose one of Justinian.[33] They also lacked an historical sense, if we may use a modern expression; they did not accept the West for what it was, and were too prone to assume an attitude of contempt. But it is evident that the West was the more at fault regarding the Roman idea transferred to Constantinople and the "unitarian" ideal embodied in the Empire. To begin with, the West fell under the domination of the barbarians and Rome itself was captured. Thus, barbarian Rome could be considered as no longer a part of the Empire, and as no longer expressing the Roman idea, which continued only in Constantinople. Better still, the West and Rome itself "went over to the barbarians" in the sense that Ozanam expressed in his famous declaration.[34] The Romans allied themselves with the enemies of the Empire as, for example, happened in the Eleventh Century with the Normans. In short, while rendering momentary homage to the Byzantine idea and to the legitimacy of the unique claims of Constantinople,[35] the West completed its betrayal by creating an Emperor supposedly Roman, but in reality Germanic and barbarian: Pope John XIII was to go so far as to write in 967, that there was "an Emperor of the Greeks" and "an Emperor of the Romans"![36]

Here the estrangement is between two worlds simultaneously political and cultural: the Byzantine world which affirms that it is the legitimate continuation of Rome, and the Latinized barbarian world, spiritually dominated by Apostolic and Papal Rome. The two worlds do not accept each other. Rome does not accept Constantinople, Constantinople does not accept the West as it is, and rather feels that this West has betrayed "the Roman idea of unity," at least as considered in Byzantium, which is to say, Roman, in the sense of Imperial.

THE DIVISION OF THE EAST AND WEST CAUSED BY THE SPREAD OF ISLAM

Let us now consider the famous thesis of Henri Pirenne[37] in his *Mohammed and Charlemagne*. In his wonted sweeping manner, his theory combines the explanation of spiritual factors with an examination of economic factors. From a commercial point of view, says Pirenne, the Carolingian epoch lags in comparison with the Merovingian epoch. What happened, essentially, was the conquest by Islam of the Mediterranean shores and the islands of Crete, Sicily and Malta, and the consequent interruption of commerce and free exchange. Instead of being a Roman-Byzantine sea, a unifying agent between the two parts of the Christian world, the Mediterranean had become a Mohammedan domain. Apart from the economic consequences that have been adduced, and the retreat of the West within a closed domain, this decisive event brought about two great happenings: a breach between East and West, and, within the West, a displacement of the economic and cultural life of the South towards the North, from the Italic and Provençal regions, that were still in contact with the Greek world, toward the territories inhabited by Germanic elements. It was in this sense that Mohammed prepared the way for Charlemagne. Thus, although the "idea of Rome" had existed until the Seventh Century despite barbarian invasions, maintaining the unity and continuity of the Roman empire, it was Islam that provoked the split which marked the end of the ancient world and the beginning of the Middle Ages.

There is certainly some truth in this thesis of Pirenne, and some Byzantine scholars have adopted it or suggested analogous considerations.[38] In recent years, however, it has drawn some very strong criticism and not only its deductions and explanations, but its economic facts themselves have been seriously questioned.[39] Navigation and commerce continued, as well as relations with the East; in Rome, the series of Oriental Popes that mark the last twenty years of the Seventh Century extended to the middle of the Eighth Century. Moreover, many other factors came into play, and the causes of the alienation already at work before Mohammed, the barbarian invasions in particular, seem to have been minimized by Pirenne.

Be that as it may, the Mohammedan expansion had important consequences in the East itself. It prevented the free communication of Eastern Christians other than those of Byzantium, and eventually of Antioch, with Rome.[40] It brought about a consolidation of Byzantium, both political and ecclesiastical; the patriarchs of Constantinople quite naturally tried to regroup under their authority the remnants of Christendom spared by the conquest.[41] Byzantium became the hope of the populations subdued by that conquest, and every armed victory of Byzantium was to the advantage of her Patriarch, and so, the national character of the Greek Church became intensified.

In any case, the Mohammedan conquest finds a place among the causes of that estrangement which in so great a measure caused the "Oriental schism."

THE CORONATION OF CHARLEMAGNE: A REPUDIATION
OF THE EAST.

For a long time the coronation of Charlemagne has been cited by Orthodox writers or controversialists among the Orthodox as one of the most decisive causes, if not *the* cause of the separation. We find this stated, for example, in a Russian polemic of the end of the Sixteenth Century which has been made known to us by "the father of Panslavism" Krijanich,[42] whose ideas are echoed in more than one page of modern writers, though in a style less violent and bombastic.[43] The importance of the coronation of Charlemagne also struck more than one Latin writer of medieval times, to say nothing of the views of Joachim of Flora who, even so, is narrow and unjust towards the Greeks.[44] Here let us give honorable mention to the remarkable report drawn up by Humbert of Romans for the Council of Union in 1274. Very realistically, Humbert places first among the three causes of discord between the Greeks and the Latins, the dispute over the empire and the various political questions that may be attached to it.[45] Modern historians, no doubt more enlightened as to the ins and outs of the question, nevertheless recognize the decisive importance of the coronation of Charlemagne.[46]

The "ins and outs" are those which we have already mentioned in regard to Constantine: the legitimacy of the succession of Constantinople to Rome as the seat of Empire and the unity of the Empire. Ever since the fall of the Empire of the West, the Emperor of Byzantium held a protective right over the Christian regions of the West—a rather theoretical guardianship which he in no way exercised, but which existed nonetheless and was recognized by the barbarian princes themselves.[47] These barbarian princes were also avid of Byzantine titles, which assimilated them to the hierarchy of the Empire—at least as avid as Bonaparte was in later centuries to be crowned by the Pope and to espouse an Austrian Archduchess. But Byzantium was careful not to bestow upon them a title which would have cast a shadow on the Imperial monarchy.[48]

As regards Byzantium therefore, the coronation on Christmas day of the year 800 was a veritable betrayal; a present-day Catholic historian has gone so far as to write:"The conferment of the Imperial title upon Charlemagne therefore marks on the part of the Pope, the intention of breaking with the Empire of the East."[49] Already in the years following 781—when the papal state was established by Pepin, the popes no longer dated their *acta* in accordance with the reign of the Emperor of Constantinople; after the year 800 they dated them from the reign of Charlemagne. From then on, a Church of Empire was to be constituted in the West, necessarily a rival to that at Byzantium. Instead of appearing as an arbiter, the pope, exposed to many acts of violence, would, from this time onward, be regarded by Constantinople as an adversary. In addition, the Latin world, sharing the same "unitarian" ideology with the East, would suffer from the eleventh-century breach consequences of apparently fearful dimensions in the direction of estrangement. The canonical authorities, who were then the authors of juridico-political theories, declared that there could be but one Emperor, as there was but one *Orbis*, and that Emperor must be Roman. The *Basileus* of Constantinople was therefore no longer the true Emperor, since he was in schism.[50]

He showed himself incapable of ensuring his function as defender of the (Roman) Church; therefore the Empire had been transferred to the Germans. Some people even declared that he no longer had the authority, that he had no *imperium*, since no authority existed outside the Church.[51] Still others were more conciliatory and pointed out that for the sake of peace, two Emperors could be allowed.[52] Actually, in the practical steps taken in the transactions to bring about union, and in the theological treatises such as that of Humbert of Romans, as well as in the pontifical bulls, the *Basileus* was still treated as Emperor.[53] In these details can be sensed all the bitterness of the question and the depth of feeling of estrangement which the coronation of Charlemagne fostered.

THE CRUSADES WIDEN THE BREACH BETWEEN EAST AND WEST.

Fleury, whose historical views are often interesting, dates the schism from the Crusades.[54] In fact, the capture of Constantinople by "the Franks"—the same who had already given themselves an Emperor—during the Fourth Crusade, created an almost irremediable situation. Up to then, there had been men of substance in the East who deemed the schism capable of being remedied and they were working toward union.[55] There would still be men of this stamp afterwards, but they would have to work in much more difficult conditions of distrust and the darkening of the atmosphere would in great part be due to the Crusades.

The facts are known. They have been studied very precisely in their relation to the anti-Latin controversy and the growth of distrust of Latins in Byzantium.[56] From the first Crusade on—though this was undertaken to aid Byzantium and doubtless as a result of its appeals—the Latins were regarded as people to fend off and to be avoided. The Emperor Alexis Comnenus had the rear guard of Bohemund attacked even before he reached Constantinople. On that occasion, the Norman warrior responded by an act of clemency and had the Greek prisoners released. The acts of hostility on the part of the Byzantines continued during the Second and the Third Crusade, going even to the extent of poisonings. Then came the Fourth Crusade, of which Venice was the evil genius. There was the double capture of Constantinople, the burning of an entire section of the town in the midst of which the Crusaders had found a mosque, there was pillage, the installation of a Latin Emperor and of a Latin patriarch and the distribution of Byzantine territories as fiefs to the Latin nobles. In short, there was all the hatefulness of an armed occupation. And there was no Semeïas to raise his voice and say:"Do not wage war upon your brothers!"[57] However, Innocent III saved the honor of the papacy and of the Christian name. Before the enterprise, he condemned it, publicly disavowing all hostile projects against the Christian Byzantines; after the capture of the city at the instigation of the Venetians, he accepted the event and saw in it a means, providentially allowed by God perhaps, to reestablish union and to group the Christian forces against the Turks. But he emphatically disavowed the outrages committed against the Byzantines.[58]

Unfortunately and against the interests of Christianity, Venice relentlessly pursued an imperialistic policy which, in all the territories of the Near East where she had established the centers of trade of her dominion, caused Latinism of the narrowest kind to reign and ruined for a long time the chances of union.[59]

The Latinization was a natural result of the Crusades wherever the Latins were able to assert themselves.[60] It is clear that at this period, which saw the development of ecclesiastical power, of canon law, and of Scholastic philosophy, the lack of an historical sense and of curiosity towards other men and other worlds gave Western Christianity that self-confidence which comprised its strength. On the other hand, it deprived the Latins of the feeling of legitimate diversity in the matter of rite, of ecclesiastical organization, of canonical tradition, and even of doctrine.[61] True, the East had likewise hardly shown an attitude of tolerance in respecting legitimate differences; the controversy of the epoch of Photius, and more especially of Cerularius, was largely based upon a condemnation of Latin usages differing from Byzantine practice, as contrary to true Christianity. With the Fourth Crusade, we enter in a period when the Latins in their turn displayed a similar exclusiveness. This was the epoch in which Innocent III compelled, as much as he could, the Bulgarian and Greek clergy to complete their ordination by the anointing with oil, though it is not a part of their rite.[62] At this same epoch the apocrisiaries of Pope Gregory IX to the Synod of Nicaea-Nymphaeum in 1233, which could have been a reunion council, demanded a rigid and unconditioned agreement with the Latin viewpoint on the two unsettled questions of the *Filioque* and azymes.[63] At this time also, Innocent IV desired the Greeks to speak in future of Purgatory "in conformity with the traditions and authority of the Holy Fathers."[64] These examples might be multiplied.[65] It is evident that, in the spiritual atmosphere of the Crusades, with little historical sense or toleration of differences, the Latins of the time considered their tradition to be *the* tradition, their formulas to be those of the very Apostles, and of the Church Fathers; it is clear as well, that by their deeds, they frequently denied the existence and legitimacy of a tradition, of a rite and of an Eastern Church. The actual measures of subordination of the Greeks to the Latins such as one finds formulated by Innocent III or Innocent IV, rather lamentably recall the situation created by colonization, when native officials are allowed some jurisdiction but are supervised by representatives of the dominating power. Thus the contact between the East and the West, resumed on the occasion and by the fact of the Crusades, turned into a new and very grave cause of estrangement. Today the memory of the Crusades still remains in the Greek mind as the memory of Latin aggression.[66]

The Greeks began to think, "Better the turban than the tiara! Anything rather than Rome." This feeling in the end influenced their behavior; "If there was a betrayal of the Christian cause, long before that of Francis I (in allying himself with the Turks,) it was the betrayal by the Orthodox in the Fifteenth Century."[67] Their responsibility is a heavy one, even though it should be understood. We are referring to another capture of Constantinople, that in 1453. This too, in a way, intensified and hardened the schism by bringing about the decadence of science and letters in Byzantium, by causing a kind of contraction and withdrawal into a national Church. This was a withdrawal which occurred everywhere in the Near East as the result of the conquest of the Turkish regime that followed. The schism was intensified, also, by the isolation in which the Orthodox world found itself, and finally by the policy pursued by the Turks, who willingly treated with the Orthodox hierarchy as the heads of national communities, while discriminating against the Latins.[68]

CONTACTS BETWEEN EAST AND WEST: MUTUAL ACCUSATIONS OF PRIDE AND ARROGANCE.

The list of politico-religious causes of the alienation is not yet ended, for contacts between Greeks (Orientals) and Latins did not cease after 1453. There were, of course, political, human and commercial contacts; there were as well, contacts with the Easterners as Christians. To give a complete and therefore a just picture, one should list the acts of true Christian fraternity, cooperation, sympathy and patience as well as the benefactions which the Latins brought constantly to the Near East in hospital, school and charitable works of all kinds, as well as in scientific and other endeavors.[69] But this is not our theme.

Real as all this was, moreover, and actual as were the events which may be cited as convicting the Easterners of a lack of gratitude, there is another very serious factor: the separated Easterners, or shall we say the Orthodox, reproach the Latins—and more precisely, Roman Catholics— for having ceaselessly exercised towards Orthodoxy a levelling and unchecked proselytism.[70] They speak of the pride of the Latins and of the Popes and their taste for domination and power.[71] The Orthodox reproach the Catholics for what they call their proselytism—a vague word which lends itself to the expression of many unreasonable rancors.

In all these reproaches, there is an approximation of truth which would not stand up before a serenely objective examination; there are many exaggerations and also quite a few candid alibis for a serious examination of conscience. But we are not trying to justify ourselves at all costs, and still less are we trying to accuse others. No matter what the circumstances, it is much better to become aware of the accusations that are brought against us, to know that they exist. We are accused of using methods of force and, instead of considering the separated Orientals as brothers whose particular gifts should be respected, of approaching them as second-rate Christians who must be won, or rather conquered, so that we may bring to them riches of which they do not have the equivalent. It is this condescension of ours, this "colonization psychology," this barely veiled desire for power, with which we are reproached. On the other hand, it is in the light of these views that, rightly or wrongly, the Eastern Christians have regarded the presence of the Latins, the contacts they have had with the West and all enterprises of the Latins, ever since the separation.

Thus, the end result of all this, especially on the part of the Orthodox and their attitude towards us, is a complex of distrust, secretly fed by all the unreasoned violence of an instinct of self-preservation. Now, there is no complex more powerful than distrust, especially when it is grafted on an *esprit de corps* and serves to justify the feeling of being different. This invalidates the clearest and soundest explanations, rendering every effort toward reconciliation ineffective, since by this standard the least sign of weakness, the lightest causes of annoyance, are seized upon as a justification for all the cherished motives for remaining apart and continuing the war.[72]

CHAPTER THREE

CULTURAL FACTORS CONTRIBUTING TO THE ESTRANGEMENT

THE DIFFERENCE OF LANGUAGE

We shall not stress the importance of language as a cultural factor, for it has long since become a classic question which has been studied so thoroughly that there is little more to be said on the matter.[1]

Yet, the question of language is important to us here, and from three points of view. A language is, to begin with, an instrument of communication. Where there is no understanding, contact becomes impossible. Thus, in Constantinople, the use of Latin was restricted to administrative and juridical formulae.[2] In the West, thanks to the monks who came from the Neapolitan region and Sicily, there were always men—especially in Rome—who understood Greek, and this language of prime importance for the sources of tradition was studied by numerous scholarly churchmen.[3] But unfortunately it is a fact that the Christian world split in two according to a line that practically corresponded to the linguistic boundary. The Greek Fathers were amazingly lacking in curiosity regarding the Latin Fathers, and the latter were scarcely better informed as to the Greeks. Such a situation was an obstacle to the true unity that lives by the exchange of ideas and by the awareness thus acquired, of the existence of ways other than one's own for approaching, and feeling, and conceiving intellectually the Holy Mysteries; and also other ways, equally legitimate, of expressing one's faith in worship and of organizing the life of the Church. The toll exacted by linguistic provincialism was bound to be, sooner or later, a certain provincialism in thought, perspective and judgment, a certain narrow separatism in the theological and canonical tradition. In short, it was bound to bring about a serious lessening of the spirit of communion and of the likelihood, if not of the very possibility, of communion.

Language is a symbol of culture and it plays a great part in the esteem civilizations have for each other. We will later return to the highly critical way in which Latins and Greeks mutually viewed each other. But, merely from the viewpoint of language itself, although the Latins were annoyed by what they considered an excess of subtlety in Greek, the Greeks themselves felt a certain condescension, if not a kind of contempt, for the Latin language.[4]

But language is not merely the symbol of ideas which would exist of themselves: language also shapes ideas. It contributes, before the thought is expressed, to the very formation of the mechanics of thought, and to the formation of that kind of inner mirror wherein our perceptions are "refracted"; it really constitutes the climate which is called "the mind."[5]

It is a fact well known to translators that for a great many words and phrases which are most expressive of profound conviction, there is no exact equivalent in another language. For example, how do we translate into any other language the German *Gemüt*, the English *worship*, the French *carrefour*, the Russian *sobornost* ? Historians of dogma, and all those working for union, are likewise well aware that many of the difficulties between the Orthodox and ourselves are linked with questions of language and that this was so in the past as it often still is today. There are the well-known instances of *prosopon*,—*hypostasis—substantia*. There are also minor instances, equally decisive; the fact that the Greeks and the Russians have generally expressed "infallibility" by the word that also signifies "impeccability" (infallible ἀναμάρτητος or in Russian *nepogrešmyĭ*), and that in Greek there is no equivalent for the Latin word *vicarius*;[6] the fact that the word αἰτία signifies "to proceed as from the first principle";[7] the fact that the word "satisfaction" practically does not exist in Greek;[8] and that, on the other hand, after having translated μετάνοια by *poenitentia*, the Latins have often joined *poenitentia* with *poena* and developed their thought in the direction of the idea of acts of penance and satisfaction.[9] These are but a few instances of many expressions that could be mentioned; while their translation is quite clear, the difficulty of achieving an exact understanding of them is likely to have serious theological and ecclesiological consequences. This language difficulty has much to do with the conditions—even with the possibilities of union, hence of unity. Their consequences lead once again to estrangement on the level of thought and mutual understanding.

VARYING DEVELOPMENT OF EASTERN AND WESTERN CULTURAL IDEALS.

The Latins considered the Greeks inordinately subtle; actually they often complained about the Greeks' quibbling and their perfidy.[10] It was the Greeks, they said, who had invented all the heresies.[11] The Greeks, for their part, accused the Latins of barbarism and lack of culture. Had not the West been overrun by the barbarians since the beginning of the Fifth Century ?[12] It has often been noted that just as Constantinople perpetuated the Roman Empire, so its schools and its culture perpetuated those of Antiquity without a break.[13] Whereas the West, after being overrun by the barbarians and resuming life with them, was in great part ignorant—with its culture being preserved by monks in small Church centers while its secular population was often illiterate—there always existed in Byzantium a cultivated laity, a corps of literate imperial functionaries.[14] Byzantium derived great advantages from this, not the least of which was, no doubt, the one pointed out by Fleury (not without a hint of gallicanism): in Byzantium the laity were more or less capable of preoccupying themselves with ecclesiastical matters; it was impossible there for the clergy to modify certain points in traditional ecclesiastical discipline, as was done in the West. Besides, and in a way as a consequence, the East experienced neither the exaggerated increase of ecclesiastical power, nor the bitter secular criticism and anticlericalism which followed and for which Fleury sets the Twelfth Century, with Arnold of Brescia, as a beginning in Western Europe.[15]

However, the question includes other aspects which are not as positive but have their bearing on the process of the gradual estrangement which we are analyzing. Without overlooking the counter-argument of "caesaropapism," of which we have already spoken and which so many Catholic writers stress, let us note at this point a very important fact which has been particularly studied by Baumstark.[16] In both the East and the West Christianity had encountered some entirely different historical presuppositions: in the East there was a millenary culture; in the West, there were barbarians and a recent culture stemming entirely from Rome. In both, West and East, there had been an invasion of new people, but under very different conditions: in the West, the Germans entered the Church, bringing with them a new vitality; in the East the Arabs, professing another faith, brought nothing into the Church but rather impelled the Greek world to withdraw into itself with its national Church. Hence, in the West, with youth and a free field, Christianity figured as a mounting force and did not hesitate to plunge into new undertakings, such as Scholasticism, a phenomenon of, and a result of youth. The West even recognized the possibility of creating a new law, based simultaneously on Rome and on the Germanic world. In the East, with its ancient culture, Christianity was held in check by Islam, and from then on figured as a force of the past, thus strengthening its traditionalism.[17]

It is relatively easy to determine the different general conditions of the development of civilization in the East and in the West. It would be less easy, especially in this limited space, to characterize adequately the content of those cultures. Restricting ourselves to the viewpoint of the Church, we will be content here to say a few words on the subject of rite—a subject which we hope to take up again one day and study more thoroughly—and to point up the differences between East and West which occurred in theological method. We shall suggest a few resulting major differences, shall recall a few moments when a feeling of profound difference, even oppositeness, was particularly marked. We shall finally note the deplorable solidification caused in the long run by so many differences, and—at least in the East—by the deep consciousness of these differences. We shall devote a section to each of these.

DIFFERENCE OF UNDERSTANDING OF "RITE"

Considered in its most limited sense, "rite" would be nothing more than an external system, no matter what its content; a certain conviction, considered as existing in itself and universally valid which could be transferred indifferently from one linguistic group to another, from one "rite" to another. Such a transfer would involve no more than a substitution of another language, different rubrics and ceremonies. On the other hand, we can understand the notion of "rite" in a much wider and deeper sense. In that case, "rite" encompasses the totality of forms and symbols by which a community gives complete expression to, and lives its Christian faith. It is then not merely a collection of liturgical rubrics but includes the theology as well as the whole manner of organization of the ecclesiastical and religious life of a people. Fundamentally then, it is the Christian life itself, collectively perceived and felt in a particular way and which creates for itself its own personal, communal manner of expression.

Now, for a long time the people and the clergy maintained a kind of profound spiritual liberty in regard to rite. It has been shown how, even in the second half of the Sixth Century and beyond into the beginnings of the Thirteenth, one passed easily from the East to the West and *vice versa*, celebrating the mass with the people of any particular place, in their language and according to their rubrics.[18] "In the Sixth Century in Rome," writes Bréhier, "when a child was brought to the baptistery, the acolyte asked: 'In what language does he confess our Lord Jesus Christ?' According to the answer, he recited the creed in Greek or in Latin."[19] Surely this state of things can be considered a wholesome pluralism. It was, however, spoiled after the Fourth Crusade as a result of Latin domination in the Orient, and the wholly Latinizing policy of Innocent III and Innocent IV.

According to Dom O. Rousseau, the Council of Florence fully recognized the existence of the Oriental rite and at the same time laid down the principle of an air-tight partition between the Greek and the Latin rites. In truth, we believe that a study of the usage of the word *ritus* leads to the following conclusion which, far from going counter to the findings mentioned above, only serves to sharpen them. Before modern times, *ritus* meant a concrete ritual, a manner of celebrating the liturgy, the concrete expression of one's faith. The Council of Florence with precisely this meaning uses the word *consuetudo*.[20] But since then—and who can say precisely when?—"rite" became an abstract reality, a thing in itself; it became a separate entity and one begins to speak of *the* Oriental Rite.

No doubt this change came about by the very reason of the separation: by reason of the Latinization, the creation of the Uniate Church, the reaction of the Orthodox and the methodical arrangement they made of their differences in the course of ten centuries of controversy, and finally in the Nineteenth Century. Today we have lost the kind of spiritual liberty which is respected in other fields, with which the variation in the manner of celebrating the liturgy was formerly treated. The question of rite has become identified with the very question of Church.

On the other hand, the East makes little or no distinction between rite and faith. In Greece, the same word, dogma, designates the one and the other. We Westerners are inured to analysis and abstraction. We conceive of faith as a body of truths which, definite in themselves, are susceptible of different expressions; we have studied the relation of symbol to reality. The Easterners see a much closer union between the two: the ritual symbol is for them but *faith in action.* Therefore, different expressions should correspond, so they think, to different faiths. They say of someone who has changed rite that he has changed faith.[21] It is a very well-known fact that in the list of grievances made by the Orthodox against the Latins, all kinds of minor variations of rite and custom have been mingled with points that are properly dogmatic, although a man such as Photius knew how to distinguish these two orders of things. Finally, and this is an important fact, in the East the Church is felt to be less an object of conviction of faith and the resulting choice, than as an actual community of peoples of which, as a Christian, one is a member.

From all this it follows that although in the West the word "rite" is taken in the narrow sense, it is understood in a broader and deeper sense in the East.[22] This brings about a type of piety that is very simple and yet very deep, not analytically developed in logical deductions and practical applications, but continually vitalized in the services of the Church, a type of piety in which the meanings of the rite, the faith, and the Church are united in a single living attitude. Possibly this involves some weaknesses; it may not perhaps respond in all points to the needs of the modern world as evolved through the ages; but it seems still more certain that such a type of piety lends itself to an exaggerated "absolute interpretation" of rite, identified with what may be held to be most absolute. In our opinion, only the reestablishment of unity and communion could restore to Christians the liberty of a kind that apparently reigned in the first six or eight centuries. In the present state of separation, there is an exaggerated tendency to "absolutize" things which are certainly important, but just as certainly not absolute: in the West there is the organization, with its administrative and juridical involvements; in the East, there is the rite.[23]

At any rate, it is in the light of these perspectives, without prejudice to other influences perhaps less sublime or even conscious, that the Orthodox peoples so severely criticise every attempt at reuniting them by giving to a Catholicism imbued with Latin spirit the mere aspect of an Oriental rite. Let us reread these lines by Father George Florovski: "There is a fatal mistake here: rite either remains merely 'ritual', incapable of bringing about reunion, the rite itself changing, becoming transformed or even degenerating into rubricism, dissipating and losing meaning; or else it is accepted in its hieratic reality, in which event, the bounds of Western or Roman consciousness must inevitably be broken. In the one case as in the other, reunion is not accomplished. In fact, Rome does not possess any of the 'Oriental rite.' What is involved is not 'rite' but the living reality of a non-Roman Christianity."[24] That is to say, there can be no Oriental rite except the Orthodox.

A rebuttal of such an assertion would require some distinctions. In a few words we can say that if "Orthodox" here signifies only Apostolic Christianity according to its Oriental tradition, the assertion may be accepted. This disposes of the subject a little cursorily, since it neglects the possibility of veritable catholicity which could be realized within the Roman Catholic Church, and in which Apostolic Christianity in its Oriental form, and according to its tradition, could co-exist with an Apostolic Christianity of Occidental tradition and form, under the primacy of the *cathedra Petri*. The Uniate Churches are, in the intention of Rome and often in reality, anticipations, preparations for this: a kind of promise, somewhat as the presence of Benjamin with Judah during the schism of the Ten Tribes, was a promise of the reunion to come.[25] However, in fact and historically, the existence of Uniate Churches and of a persevering effort of Rome to organize them, has been felt by the separated Eastern Christians as a veritable betrayal, as a lack of respect towards the East, as a refusal to take seriously—or a congenital inability to take seriously—their reasons for not aligning themselves with a Latinized Catholicism: in short, to take seriously the reasons for estrangement that the present study is attempting to analyze. In our opinion, it is quite certain that many sentimental complexes, irrational rather than rational, are intermixed with all this. However, it is a fact—and one would be wrong not to take it into serious consideration—that Uniatism appears to the Orthodox as being, by its profound presuppositions, the very caricature and contradiction of unity.[26]

SCHOLASTICISM IN THE WEST AND THE DIFFERENCE OF THEOLOGICAL METHOD.

Theological method and major differences in doctrinal conceptions are other factors to be considered. Dom Wilmart, a profound student of ancient texts, has written that a Christian of the Fourth or Fifth Century would have felt less bewildered by the forms of piety current in the Eleventh Century than would his counterpart of the Eleventh Century in the forms of the Twelfth. The great break occurred in the transition period from the one to the other century.[27] This change took place only in the West where, sometime between the end of the Eleventh and the end of the Twelfth Century, everything was somehow transformed. This profound alteration of view did not take place in the East where, in some respects, Christian matters are still today what they were then—and what they were in the West before the end of the Eleventh Century. This is a statement that becomes clearer the better one knows the facts. It is indeed very serious, for it concerns precisely the moment when the schism asserted itself in a way that has been without a true remedy up to now. It seems impossible that this be a purely exterior and fortuitous coincidence. Perhaps, it is much more likely that we have come to the very core of our subject. However, with the idea of returning elsewhere to it some day, we will not now treat this immense and fascinating subject as a whole, but merely from the theological point of view and to begin with, from the actual state of theology, without however, supplying detailed and elaborated proofs.

In the period between the end of the Eleventh Century and the end of the Twelfth, a decisive turning-point was reached in the West. It was a time characterized by several transitions. There was first, the transition from a predominantly essential and exemplarist outlook to a naturalistic one, an interest in existence. This was a transition from a universe of exemplary causality, in which the expressions of thought or of act receive their truth from the transcendent model which material things imitate, to a universe of efficient causality in which the mind seeks for the truth in things and in their empirical formulations. Secondly, there was the transition "from a symbol to dialectic,"[28] or, as one might say with greater precision, from a synthetic perception to an inclination for analysis and "questions." Here we have the beginning of Scholasticism, to which so many scholars have devoted their talents.[29] This, it seems to us, is the essential point. The difference between the two worlds is the difference between the attitude of synthetic perception in quest of the relation of the parts to the whole, and an analytical attitude. Basically, was it not against this analytical attitude of Catholics that the Slavophile religious philosophy aimed its criticism of Catholicism, in the Nineteenth Century?[30]

Another transition was that from a culture where tradition reigned and the habit of synthesis became ingrained, to an academic milieu where continual questioning and research was the norm, and analysis the normal result of study. The East followed the road of tradition, and we have shown how one of the principal differences among the various peoples of the Orthodox faith is in fact that they are not trained, as are the Latins, by the schools.[31] The Latin theologians, inured to Scholasticism, have often been baffled at seeing the Greeks refuse to yield to their compelling arguments from reason, but instead taking refuge in the realm of Patristic texts and conciliar canons, as Humbert of Romans very pertinently remarked.[32] The times had greatly changed since the period when the Greeks treated the Latins as barbarians; now the so-called barbarians had created a new science, full of developments which have made the modern world. But this remained foreign to the East which knew no Scholasticism of its own,[33] and was to experience neither the Reformation or the 16th-18th-century rationalism. In other words, the East remained foreign to the three influences that shaped modern Catholicism. Therefore, the West has evolved towards a type of analytical knowledge which, in sum, is rational; it *needs to* define the exact shape of things, to see them independently of one another. In the period that we have been studying, or rather at a slightly later time, the first half of the Thirteenth Century, a new kind of theological teaching and study appeared and established itself in the West. Until this time, the dominant type of teaching or study had been of a contemplative or monastic nature, linked with the liturgical life of the abbeys or cathedrals. Now, there was added a new type of teaching and study, of an academic and rational nature which was soon to take the place of the former. Here the significant incident is that of Abailard leaving the cloister of Notre-Dame to go to Mont Ste. Geneviève, where our great schools arose.

In the East, on the other hand, the teaching and study of theology, and even of philosophy, kept its religious status. It was only in the neo-Orthodox school of which Fr. Serge Bulgakov was the most accomplished representative, that sapiential knowledge was neither a separate philosophy nor a pure mystique, nor a "scientific" theology, but all three combined.[34] It was not only among the Slavophiles that the idea of an integral and living knowledge was proposed, within the epistemological structure in which love and moral uprightness meet and join.[35] As far as we know, this may be a general characteristic of the Byzantine philosophy itself.[36] The Orthodox Slavs have a distrust, if not contempt, for the "rational," the "Euclidean," as Dostoevsky says, considering them "extrinsic" or "worldly" (the famous Russian *vnešnost'*), which may not be entirely fortunate or of positive value. It is possible that half a century of the Marxist regime will bring Russian Orthodoxy in one bound to the point which we have reached through seven centuries of analysis and rationalism. They will, of course, cover the road in the continuity and spirit of Orthodox tradition, but perhaps Orthodoxy will thus be brought a little closer to us. For the moment, it is in a climate of living knowledge and negation. Just as the Latins in general feel the need to define —especially Rome, which has the calling and charism to effect this—so the Orientals feel *the need not* to define: not to define, be it noted, even the beliefs they hold in common with us. The example of the Assumption of the Virgin Mary is significant in this respect.[37]

It is a fact that many points of doctrine have not been decided in the Orthodox East and that various positions were, and indeed still are, occasionally upheld there, sometimes even the Catholic position. Jugie felt that he could deduce from this that reunion should be easy since, in the state of doctrinal uncertainty in which they find themselves, the Orthodox churches could admit the definitions already accepted in our Church, definitions which have for us the force of dogmatic law.[38] But is this not treating the Orientals precisely as if they were Latins? For the point is not exactly that they do not have definitions; the point is rather that *they do not need them*, do not want them at all. One cannot straightaway employ as a means of union that which precisely constitutes one of the obstacles to union. We must all the more take into account the *ethos* of the Oriental Churches, their *pietas*, we might say, recalling the similar case of the Anglicans, to whom this word means so much, representing so many things that cannot be defined and which, on a religious plane, are analogous to culture—if it is true that, according to a famous remark, culture is what remains when we have forgotten everything else.

This indeterminate state of things is, however, valuable from the viewpoint of reunion, and Jugie's idea involves a great truth to which we should pay careful attention. Orthodoxy has kept itself malleable and retains possibilities which might crystallize into a favorable position towards reunion, a position which, however, it would be folly to force from the outside. In studying Eastern thought in all its diversity and ramifications, or at least its expressions on a certain number of things as important to union as the subject of Purgatory or the Roman primacy,[39] we personally have been amazed to note that there is a broad and deep domain of ideas wherein the East and the West cherish a fundamentally common tradition. In the apparently vast area where definitions exist among us, but not in the East, it has happened that theologians and Churchmen of the East have sometimes expressed themselves in a manner widely divergent from, if not totally opposed to, the Western position, and again, in a thoroughly Catholic sense, or very close to it. This has happened especially in moments that were favorable to reunion, or has come from men who were favorably disposed toward reunion.

Catholic apologists are fond of quoting and using these favorable texts, and they are right to do so. Yet we would no longer follow them if, once again, their secret design were to abolish any and all differences between the Eastern and the Western tradition, to the advantage of Latin Catholicism. On the other hand, we would like to stress a very important point to which we will return in our conclusion to this study: the schism, the "estrangement," has not been brought to completion. It is possible that it could become complete if we were to push to the limit the differences which, explained intelligently, could smooth the path to reunion. (The question of the *Filioque* is a case in point.) On the other hand, we might halt the movement toward total schism and work towards a healing of the wound whenever, faithful to what we hold to be the truth, we seek and find on the level of thought and then on the level of formulae, an acceptable view which tends towards reunion.

Understandably, we cannot risk the choice of deepening the estrangement instead of achieving a rapprochement and a profound unity on the basis of the famous pronouncement of St. Cyprian: "licet, salvo jure communionis, diversum sentire."[40] Everything is fundamentally common to the East and the West, and yet everything is different. We have elsewhere suggested that, loosely speaking, a great many of these differences may be due to the platonic line of thought followed in the East, and the aristotelian one followed in the West, without, of course, any technical or historical dependence on either Plato or Aristotle.[41] But we trust no one expects us to insert at this point a chapter on comparative symbolism.

THE SOLIDIFICATION OF DIVERGENT WAYS OF THINKING

These cultural and religious differences are very important; consequently, even where the fundamental positions are identical, still almost everything is different because differently felt, interpreted, construed, expressed and experienced. That is why we have given so much space to these elements in our book, *Divided Christendom*.[42] The extremely interesting criticism raised by Vl. Lossky, which we have since taken into account, has not shaken our actual convictions confirmed since by so many facts, and which are likewise the convictions of some excellent experts and friends of the East.[43] We wish that all Catholics would become aware of these factors and their importance; we wish they might enter into a sympathetic and patient consideration of the spirit of the East and, since we must face it, the spirit of Orthodoxy. This is the main reason why we have welcomed a number of works on the Slavophile movement into our French collection, *Unam sanctam*.

It is not a question of abolishing these differences, but it is imperative that we do not elevate them to an absolute. We have seen in the matter of rite, how this danger is not merely imaginary. Moreover, the danger presents itself in slightly different ways in the East and in the West.

On the Catholic side, there is the danger of reconciling a Latinism in fact with a catholicity of intention; there is the danger of practically identifying part of the Christian tradition with that tradition as a whole, and this in matter of piety and theological thought. We say "a part of the Christian tradition," and mean by this not its Western form alone but a period of that tradition—for example its scholastic or medieval or baroque period, or its period of administrative centralization, or similar instances. It is quite a natural tendency to mistake "accepted" ideas for tradition!

On the part of the Orientals, or more precisely the Orthodox, the danger lies in identifying true Christianity with the Orthodox Church, not only dogmatically but with its national and Eastern forms as such. The conscience of Christianity tends to be identified with the conscience of the East itself, and the East, as such, becomes, by definition, pure, holy, profound, and blessed by God.[44] Many times, when talking to an Orthodox, have I felt the unconscious attitude of one who has a fixed point of reference for all his perceptions and which could be explained like this: what is Western is insipid, superficial, exterior, mechanical; what is Eastern is profound, interior, living. . . .

For a great many peoples of the Near East, the Church— not only the Orthodox, but also the Nestorian or Monophysite—has represented a national refuge; it is in the Church that they have preserved their national peculiarities despite the various invaders and conquerors to whom they have been subject. The consequences have been a strengthening of national characteristics and the hemming-in of Christianity within national and ethnical boundaries. As the late lamented Dom Clement Lialine said, making a play on the French word *pierre* (rock=Peter), "Just as the Catholics have been accused of 'rock-like insensibility,' so the Orthodox could be accused of 'rock-like incuriosity.'"[45] In Russia, where this has played a smaller part, and the Orthodox Church has been closely and almost inextricably linked to the national life, the continuity has been so strong that even the Bolshevik regime has not succeeded in breaking it. Besides, the Slavophiles of the Nineteenth Century systematized with remarkable profundity the sentiment of identification between a whole people—the Russians— and true Christianity. Slavophiles benefitted by the contributions of German Romanticism and Idealism, of the German idea of a *Volksgeist*, which the Slavophiles transposed into a highly spiritual theology of the Church wherein the people themselves—the Orthodox Russian people—are the bearers of truth and holiness.[46] It seems clear to us, at least, that the Slavophiles have erected into absolutes the Eastern and national elements, at least as they are conceived by them and highly idealized. The criticism of Soloviev is to a great extent well founded.[47] Every reader of Dostoevsky knows that in his writings this has been carried to the point of an idolatry of "Russian Christianity" and of "the Russian God."[48] It was towards the end of the Nineteenth Century and following the new ways opened by the Slavophiles, that anthropological differences and religious peculiarities were sytematized. Prince Eugene Troubetskoy seems to have been the first to do it with scope and penetration.[49] Aside from a whole literature on "the Russian Soul," all of this has had the result of increasing and crystallizing the consciousness of being quite different from the Westerners, and in many respects has even widened the breach.

It is clear that such "absolutisations" of local and cultural elements would destroy all possibility of one day reuniting the separated communities into one communion. Assuredly, the accentuation of cultural peculiarities has been both the cause and the effect of schism. The late lamented Dom Nicholas Oehmen[50] analyzed with great theological perspicacity the way in which it was the fatal cause of schism. Israel, chosen to be the people of God, was not noted for its high culture; men were called to unite themselves (ecclesia) in pure faith in the Word, in the pure grace of Jesus

Christ, in short, they were called upon to adhere to a supra-human, supra-rational, supra-cultural plan. The divisions result-ed from the fact that elements of a cultural and human order were brought into religion, such as Hellenism, Latin temperament, Scholasticism, and others. From this point of view, the schisms are linked together as in a chain, and one might say that the schism of the Sixteenth Century would not have occurred had there not been the schism of the Eleventh Century, and that the latter in turn would not have occurred had there not been the first breach, the one by which the Christian Church left the human pov-erty of the people of God for the human wealth of nations.

Much indeed, could be said on this subject. It is possible to visualize, as we have done in *Divided Christendom*, the work of unification being carried out within a truly Catho-lic framework and this with an amplitude that would admit the possiblility of contributions from all peoples and all cul-tures. At least the problem has been stated in all its force.

CHAPTER FOUR

ECCLESIOLOGICAL FACTORS
CONTRIBUTING TO THE ESTRANGEMENT

FROM EARLIEST TIMES, THE CONCEPT OF
TWO ECCLESIASTICAL WORLDS

Two ecclesiastical worlds, a duality, have asserted themselves ever since the time of Constantine--if not from the very beginnings: "uterque orbis," as Pope St. Simplicius was to write.[1] If we were to trace the development of this duality in this state of mutual ignorance and estrangement, the acceptance of which really constitutes the schism, we would have to rewrite the whole history of the two churches. Here I can only stake out the terrain, indicating significant landmarks rather than give a complete documentation. In the year of 342 "the first great manifestation of antagonism between the two halves of Christiantiy"[2] took place during the Council of Sardica (now Sofia). Not that the Council was purely Western in composition,[3] as it has sometimes been said, but it remained on the periphery of the two worlds, within the area of Western obedience: at the Council, Latin was spoken, the acts were first drawn up in Latin, but their Greek translator significantly enough, transformed or toned down the implications of the canon which cited Rome as supreme.[4] Not only were the two doctrinal positions in opposition--that of the Westerners being saner--but two groups of church leaders and two ways of conceiving the canonical regime of life or of Church union were opposing each other.

The crisis and the quarrel aroused by Arianism gave both the East and the West the opportunity to note that they did not have the same preoccupations, the same way of reasoning. There began to be held two parallel councils as at Sardica: so, for instance, in 359, when the Council of Rimini and that of Seleucia Trachea were held simultaneously. As we have seen from the number of periods during which Constantinople and Rome broke off communion between the years 323 and 787, or between 337 and 843, it is clear that a kind of "separateness" had become a kind of habit.

It was in the atmosphere of this latent rupture that the complicated and interminable episodes of the schism of Antioch took place[5] in spite of the noble attempt of St. Basil to find a unanimity under the aegis of Rome. What was at the bottom of this affair? Questions of personalities, of strictness in matter of orthodoxy, or in matters concerning personal qualities or, as Cavallera thinks, a misunderstanding as to the way of conceiving ecclesiastical discipline? In any case, long interruptions of communion ensued, often only partial and not always continuing, since a given see sometimes remained in communion with either of two churches in schism with each other. And once again, parallel and discordant councils were held at Constantinople and at Rome in 382. It was in this rather unfavorable atmosphere that the name of "Constantinople, the second Rome," acquired its official and canonical existence, sanctioned by the Council of Constantinople in 381. In short, the East and the West were separated.[6] Even if we do not stress the indications,

with Cavallera, of a marked anti-Western trend on the part
of the Eastern Church--in this case the Syrians--there remains
the fact that the "relations between the Church of the East
and the Church of the West, during the last third of the
Fourth Century, had already crystallized as strained. On the
part of the one and the other, there were misunderstandings,
disagreements and lack of sympathy despite a sincere desire
for concord."[7]

The reactions were often different in the East and the
West in regard to the 5th-century heresies: Pelagianism and
questions of grace,[8] Christological difficulties, Nestorianism,
and Monophysitism. Before and especially after the Council of Chalcedon, the East was prone to react in the Alex-
andrian way, that is to say, to show itself more favorable
toward Monophysitism; the West always wanted to save,
if one may so express it, the portion of the Nestorian truth
consecrated by Chalcedon. The resistance to the condem-
nations of the Three Chapters desired by Justinian (Theo-
dora) unified Africa, Italy and Illyricum.[9] The different
ways of approaching the unique mystery of Christ in the
East and the West—the one putting a more lively value on
the acts of his humanity, the other on a line of descent from
celestial realities to the midst of the sensible word—were
bound to have correspondences or consequences in liturgy
and ecclesiology. In the Orient there developed a rather
sumptuous liturgy, imbued with the Holy Mysteries and the
idea of "Heaven on Earth." It was a church essentially
sacramental, a church of prayer with less attention to the
exigencies of its militant and its itinerant state. The West,
especially Rome, held to a more sober liturgy which was
aimed at the edification of the individual and his moral

needs.[10] This was a church much more effectively marked by the sytem of militant action and the human expression of the spiritual-celestial authority—that of Peter and that of Christ.

At a time when Rome was more and more finding and accepting a co-existence with the Western, that is to say, the barbarian powers, Constantinople was becoming more and more Oriental. Dvornik has noted some significant indications of this fact, particularly in observing which churches were represented at the councils of the Seventh, Eighth and Ninth Centuries.[11] Illyricum, Greek in language but Roman in patriarchical obedience, was conspicuously absent from them. We have already pointed out that, after Heraclius (610-641), in the course of the concentration and renovation undergone by the Byzantine Empire in consequence of the Arab peril, there took place a more complete Hellenization and nationalization of the Church under the rule of the Patriarch of Constantinople, whose influence increased.[12] Following the Iconoclast crisis in the mid-Eighth Century, the quarrel was intensified and the politico-religious breach widened. The Emperors used Iconoclasm as a means of controlling the Church. (The *Ecloge* of the Emperor Leo III in 776 opens with a declaration in which he applies to himself the text of John XXI,15 and following).[13] This occurred at the moment when Frankish protection was offered to the papacy and brought to it the material basis of its independence of the *Basileus*. Through all this, the disaffection and estrangement of the two *orbis* became tragically complete. However, the iconophiles who had found support in Rome from Pope Gregory II and had partially triumphed thanks to his support, submitted to an Occidental

Council the Canons of the Seventh Ecumenical Council—
the last which East and West held in common—of the year
787. Unfortunately, the new protector of the papacy, Charlemagne, ruined this chance for unanimity (The *Libri Carolini*
and the Council of Frankfurt in 790 and 794). It is true
that the Acts of the Seventh Council had been transmitted
to Charlemagne in a poor version and that the Pope had
delayed approving them by reason of the caesaropapism
which was mingled in them. Charlemagne was also guilty
of having deepened the mutual distrust. For it was likewise
the period when he imposed the *Filioque* upon the churches
of his empire and went so far as to refuse the *per Filium* in
the *Libri Carolini*, thus giving for a long time credence in
the Greek mind to the idea that the Latins allow two principles of the Holy Ghost and that the formula of several Eastern Fathers, a formula which the Council of Florence was
to recognize as possibly equivalent in meaning to the *Filioque*, was in reality opposed to it. Thus, Khomiakov and the
Slavophiles date from this period the "moral fratricide" and
the beginning of the rupture which they attribute entirely
to the West![14] Yet Pope Adrian I defended the Seventh
Ecumenical Council against the *Libri Carolini* as well as the
procession of the Holy Ghost "a Patre per Filium"; Pope
Leo III, confronting the envoys of Charlemagne, held the
position which was to be that of many Orientals: legitimacy
of the doctrine, illegitimacy of the addition of the *Filioque*.
He then caused to be engraved and placed before the tomb
of St. Peter two silver placques bearing the text of the Creed,
the one in Latin, the other in Greek, without the *Filioque*.[15]

THE LOGIC OF EVENTS CAUSES THE DEVELOPMENT
OF CONSTANTINOPLE
AS AN AUTONOMOUS PATRIARCHATE

Throughout an entire history of which we have recalled just a few episodes, but which is, as a whole, the history of gradual estrangement, the Metropolitans of Constantinople increased their influence and developed what many Western historians call their pretensions or ambitions. It is a history often retraced since it is regarded as the most decisive chapter in the preparation and causes of the schism itself.[16] Certain Orthodox historians, for their part, admit that the ambitions of the Patriarchs of Constantinople were partially responsible for the schism.[17] The schism had, indeed, begun from the moment that there could be constituted a Patriarchate of Constantinople in a national Church, coextensive with the political jurisdiction of the Emperor. Significantly enough, Hergenröther commences his authoritative work, *Photius, sein Leben, seine Schriften und das griechische Schisma* (1867-69), with the founding of Constantinople. It seems hardly debatable that thenceforth an implacable logic drove the Church of Constantinople towards an autonomy independent of any other ecclesiastical metropolis, and towards playing a dominant role in the Eastern portion of Christianity. Moreover, other cities argued at one time or another that they had been, or still were, imperial residences, in order to claim an independence: so, for example, Milan and Aquileia (*Roma secunda*); and why not Ravenna, Arles, Trèves, or Aix-la-Chapelle, which was called "new Rome" in the poetry of the time of Charlemagne?[18]

This pretension of Constantinople is inscribed not only in the events but in the canonical texts. The sequence of the latter is so well known that we may be excused if we do not go into detail. There was, first of all, the Council of Constantinople in 381:

> That the Bishop of Constantinople holds primacy of rank (*Tὰ πρεσ-βεῖα τῆς τιμῆς*) after the Bishop of Rome, because Constantinople is the new Rome.[19]

Then we have the famous canon 28 of the Council of Chalcedon in 451:

> Following in all things the decrees of the Holy Fathers and recognizing the Canon of the 150 bishops beloved of God, the said canon having been read, we also, being of the same mind, decree and accord equally the same prerogative (*περὶ τῶν πρεσβείων*) to the Holy Church of Constantinople, the new Rome. It was with justice indeed that the Fathers had granted to Old Rome the prerogatives it enjoyed because that city is the place where the Emperor reigns. Moved by the same considerations, the 150 bishops have decided that the new Rome, which now has the honor of being the seat of Empire and of the Senate and enjoys, on the civilian plane, privileges equalling those of the ancient imperial Rome, shall have the same privileges in the ecclesiastical order, and be second only to Rome."[20]

We know what St. Leo's reaction was on the subject of the 28th Canon: "In irritum mittimus et per auctoritatem B. Petri apostoli, generali prorsus definitione cassamus."[21] Thus the Pope reacted against the principle that assimilated the ecclesiastical order to the political one.[22] But, as Wuyts has well shown (see Note 20 *supra*), he especially reacted in the name of the ancient tradition establishing the ecclesiastical order of itself on the canonical plane (Canon 6 of Nicaea). His Holiness Pope Pius XII noted that the 28th Canon of Chalcedon did not fundamentally go counter to the Roman primacy, and that it was for other reasons that St. Leo rejected it. The reaction of the Pope had its effect, since the Slavic *Nomocanon* in the Ninth Century expressly omits our Canon because of St. Leo's refusal to sanction it.[23] Practically, however, no attention was paid in Byzantium to this reaction or to the way—in truth, rather debatable— in which Rome constructed its vision of the *Apostolic* regime of the Church, herself flourishing and strong, beginning with the Apostle Peter.[24] The Metropolitan of Constantinople to whom Rome for a long time avoided even giving the title of Patriarch,[25] later refusing to recognize the title of "Ecumenical Patriarch, —that is, "principal" or perhaps "imperial"—[26] continued to increase and affirm the primacy of his rank as well as his prestige, independence, and real influence over all churches of the Byzantine Empire.[27] The legal texts continued after the Council of Chalcedon, such as Novella 131 of Justinian (March 18, 545),[28] or the Second Quinisext Council of Trullo (692).[29] One might say that the idea of the Patriarch of Constantinople ranking immediately after the Bishop of ancient Rome was fixed in the consciousness of the East.

Rome, for her part, accepted this idea only reluctantly and without giving to it the exact meaning it had in Byzantium. And Rome, while holding out against the pretensions of the Patriarch, unceasingly pursued the struggle against those of the Emperor, setting Apostolic principles against the politico-religious principle in the conception of the life of the Church. Though sometimes expressed with regrettable bluntness, and a lack of preciseness in wording and even by the use of formulae that were themselves debatable, the Apostolic principle and the correlative theory of the distinction of powers as Pope Gelasius defined them, animated the Roman attitude in the course of the numerous crises which, until the fatal date of 1054, set her in opposition to Constantinople.

The painful points are familiar: as always, they brought about a truly irreconcilable opposition when political interests or questions of influence became entangled with religious questions (as in usages and liturgy), canonical matters (as in the affair of the fourth marriage of Emperor Leo VI the Wise, [886-912]), or points of dogma such as Iconoclasm or the various imperial heresies. This was particularly the case for the question of Illyricum, a latent irritation ever since the Fourth Century, which became acute in the Eighth Century during the Iconoclast dispute, when Constantinople annexed what remained of the province, and later, when the Bulgarian difficulty added fuel to the conflict between Photius and Rome.[30] Thus, Constantinople had accomplished her aim of making her ecclesiastical domain coincide with the political and cultural domain of the Empire. The logic was to be carried through to its ultimate conclusion, that is, to the claim of an independent and therefore sovereign authority; and to the point of the estrangement of two worlds, two *orbis*. But since the schism was realized in the minds and hearts of men before it entered into events and formal declarations, we must now, before describing the final episode of the separation, trace the main lines of a secular opposition to the canonico-theological concept of the organization and administration of ecclesiastical life.

TWO THEORIES OF THE CHURCH FOUNDED NOT ON DOGMA BUT ON CANONICAL TRADITION.

It must be clearly specified at what level the two theories of the Church differ. The difference is not, first of all, on the dogmatic level. There is an idea of the Church as the body of Christ, as communication of the faith through the catechism and baptism, then of sanctifying grace through the other sacraments, supremely the Eucharist; this idea is the same in both the East and the West. This identity of belief extends to the sacramental and hierarchical structure of the Church, to the respective positions of the priesthood and the faithful in regard to the sources of sanctification.[31] Briefly, *the mystery of the Church* is fundamentally the same in both the East and the West.

Therefore, is it right to see, as Zankov does,[32] for example the conceptual differences of the two ecclesiologies as the cause of the breach? Doubtless, the author professes a "neo-orthodox" theology of the Church, a theology which some would call "modernist," or shall we say precisely, Slavophile, and perhaps he unduly traces this concept back to the Tenth Century. Let us study the question more closely: here is our hypothesis, based on the study of the historical development of ecclesiology, especially in the West, a study the results of which we hope some day to present elsewhere. The *theology* of the mystery of the Church, both in the West and in the East, may be summed up as a point of view on the constitution and administration of the Church, a "polity" of the Church, as it was called in the Sixteenth and Seventeenth Centuries. This point of view is expressed in the canonical declarations. Now, although the mystery of the Church is fundamentally the same in the East and the West, yet two different canonical traditions developed independently in the East and in the West; very soon, and with ever greater force, they were in opposition to each other and clashing.[33] The clash was all the more irremediable since, in both the East and the West, the canonical determinations involved a certain theological interpretation and outlook as to the Church and so, they took on dogmatic value. This was especially so in the West, where the principal and decisive question of this practical ecclesiology—the primacy and infallibility of the Roman See— became the focal point of ecclesiology and finally received a formal dogmatic definition.

Such, in a few words, is the drama that we will have to unfold in this section. We will first of all present the development of the Eastern tradition, then that of the Roman and Catholic position; but it must be remembered that, historically, these two developments were concomitant and produced that progressive alienation, that decisive estrangement, the acceptance of which, we repeat—with some qualification which will be given in our last chapter—represents *the very reality of the schism.*

The East: misunderstanding of how the West conceived the Primacy.

It is a fact that the East recognized the primacy of the Bishop of Rome. Doubtless not entirely with the meaning and to the degree that we are led to believe by certain Catholic writings, but much more widely than the Orthodox today are willing to admit. These present-day members of the Orthodox faith are apparently held back by their determination not to admit the modalities and consequences of the primacy as developed by the Roman Church and by their refusal even to admit what is historically and categorically attested. Here again it is impossible to give a full account of the two positions, since even a summary would require a whole volume. We refer the reader to those studies that exist[34] and will here merely give the argument in outline.

To begin with, let us recognize that a good number of facts proposed as proof demonstrate no more than the Orthodox of today would not refuse to admit. This is particularly true of the "appeals to Rome," or the laws handed down by the *Basileis*. The appeals were often not addressed to the Pope alone; for instance, Origen did not submit his orthodoxy to Fabian alone, but to other bishops as well; St. John Chrysostom addressed himself to Milan and Aquileia as well as to Rome; and the Emperor Leo VI submitted the question of his fourth marriage to the other Patriarchs as well as to the Pope. Again, the appeals sometimes presupposed nothing other than the position of the *prima sedes*, of which there never was any question.

On the other hand, we see Rome affirming her primacy throughout the centuries without this causing the East to break off communion or denounce an abuse. Let us admit the debatable point,[35] that the very forceful texts of Pope Siricius, (384-398), of Pope Innocent I (401-417), of Pope Zosimus (417-418), and of Pope Boniface (418-422) are aimed directly at the East.[36] The fact remains that Pope Julius I (337-352) voided a Council held in the East, and that Athanasius submitted to this judgment; there remain the universal and unconditional claims of St. Leo (440-461)[37] and of Gelasius; there remains the famous Formula of Hormisdas (515) to which the bishops of the East, perhaps unwillingly, subscribed at the end of the schism of Acacius;[38] and there remain the affirmations of St. Gregory the Great which the Patriarch John IV ("The Faster") and Cyriacus admitted, although the Pope reprimanded them strongly. (See note 26, *supra*). In the impressive mass of writings and facts assembled by Jugie to demonstrate that the East recognized the Roman primacy, a great number of them which concern the Fourth and Fifth Centuries, in particular the Great Councils of the period, seem to be conclusive.[39] The testimonies continued after the Seventh Century: that of St. Theodore of Studion († 826) is famous, and that of his contemporary, St. Nicephorus, Patriarch of Constantinople, deserves to be no less so.[40] They even continued to a certain degree after the schism, if indeed the texts cited by our authors will bear the sense attributed to them.[41]

However, it must be confessed that the consciousness of the Roman primacy was not expressed in the East at the period when that primacy became classically fixed in tradition, at least not with a clarity that alone could have avoided schism. In the great councils held in the East, there had never been a formula on the universal primacy by divine right. Many of the Eastern Fathers who are rightly acknowledged to be the greatest and most representative and are, moreover, so considered by the Universal Church, do not offer us any more evidence of the primacy. Their writings show that they recognized the primacy of the Apostle Peter, that they regarded the See of Rome as the *prima sedes* playing a major part in the Catholic communion—we are recalling, for example, the writings of St. John Chrysostom and of St. Basil who addressed himself to Rome in the midst of the difficulties of the schism of Antioch—but they provide us with no theological statement on the universal primacy of Rome by divine right. The same can be said of St. Gregory Nazianzen, St. Gregory of Nyssa, St. Basil,[42] St. John Chrysostom,[43] St. John Damascene.[44] We do not find texts in the East as strong as those in the West; the rescripts of Theodore and of Valentinian II and Valentinian III concern the

West. In a number of documents Rome is merely portrayed as an ecclesiastical and canonical court of first instance. In other texts, Rome is recognized as having the right as first See, of intervening to preserve the purity of doctrinal tradition, but not to regulate the life of the churches or to settle questions of discipline in the East. Finally—and to our mind this is the most important point—although the East recognized the primacy of Rome, it did not imply by this exactly what Rome herself did, so that, even within the question on which they were in agreement, there existed the beginning of a very serious estrangement bearing upon the decisive element of the ecclesiastical constitution and the rule of communion.

Batiffol has summed up all this very well:

> I believe that the East had a very poor conception of the Roman primacy. The East did not see in it what Rome herself saw and what the West saw in Rome, that is to say, a continuation of the primacy of St. Peter. The Bishop of Rome was more than the successor of Peter on his *cathedra*, he was Peter perpetuated, invested with Peter's responsibility and power. The East has never understood this perpetuity. St. Basil ignored it, as did St. Gregory Nazianzen and St. John Chrysostom. In the writings of the great Eastern Fathers, the authority of the Bishop of Rome is an authority of singular grandeur, but in these writings it is not considered so by divine right. It is regrettable that so fundamental an issue was not settled by full discussion and by an ecumenical council during the centuries when there was still union.[45]

Despite this difference in the content of ideas, despite the opposite positions taken—the Romans with their thesis of supreme apostolic power attached to Peter, the Greeks with their leanings towards an Imperial Church regulated by the canonical systems more or less subordinate to the *Basileus*—a *modus vivendi* was established. The expression is, we believe, that of L. Bréhier;[46] it has proven popular and the idea has been taken up by several Catholic historians.

Batiffol has proposed the very enlightening idea of three zones in which the papal *potestas* was exercised: (1) a zone around the city of Rome, immediately subject to Rome, (2) the zone of the West outside of Italy, and (3) a zone of universal extension but concretely representing the East where Rome only intervened, but with authority, as arbiter of the whole communion and as judge in *causae majores*.[47]

Even at the most brilliant epoch of the Roman primacy, that of St. Leo (440-461) to which the subsequent epochs added very little, that was the state of things; St. Leo wanted to avoid the possibility of Constantinople's isolating herself and becoming a completely autonomous center in the East,[48] but he allowed the Eastern churches to administer themselves and intervened only in affairs which placed Catholic unity in question.[49] While struggling for the principle of the *Kirchenführung* that should be apostolic and deriving from Peter instead of being politico-local, Rome finally came to accept many things on the part of the Emperor and of the Patriarch of Constantinople.[50] Dvornik has shown, principally on the basis of the Council of 861, that Photius had admitted the Roman primacy as imbedded in our *modus vivendi*: administrative and canonical autonomy of the local churches under the rule of the Universal Church, assured by a canonical primacy of Rome. This was exercised in the appeals to Rome and the judgment by the Pope and his legates of the canonical debates of the East.[51] It was a regime of this type, with a more precise recognition of the primacy, that Innocent III himself approved for the Bulgarians.[52]

Thus we find a certain duality in the exercise of the primacy: There were, moreover, frequent interventions, as well as the exercise of the role of arbiter which involved a true and proper power of jurisdiction. The Christian optimism of Bréhier in the study cited above makes him consider the continuation of such a *modus vivendi* or even its eventual reestablishment quite possible and almost easily achieved.[53] Perhaps this results from not seeing quite clearly enough that beneath the duality of the regime there was in reality an ambiguity of canonical and ecclesiological views. The development of the consciousness of the primacy in Rome and in the West, with the even stronger affirmation that it entailed, caused this ambiguity to be tragically revealed,[54] and the dogmatic definition pronounced since then in the Catholic Church, makes it henceforth impossible to be overlooked. Before examining the ideas that prevailed in Rome and in the West let us try to grasp the point of view of the East.

Once more we must go back to the Council of Sardica, which we have already seen was the first great manifestation of the estrangement on the plane of the Church as such. Sardica was an attempt by the West to canonize the regulatory role of Rome. Now, if it would be inexact to believe that Sardica was in no way accepted in the East,[55] it still is true that it did not play the same part there, as in the West, where its canons were for a long time confounded with those of Nicaea, indeed were still so confounded until the time of St. Leo, and this despite the discussion begun in 419 between Rome and Carthage.[56] The cause of the estrangement was that some authorities considered certain canons which regulated appeals to Rome to apply to the whole Church —and in reality they were hardly ever applied in the West— and others gave them no such value.

The canons reflect certain interpretations and a certain way of conceiving things. Now, as we have seen, the East did not feel quite the same as the West did about the Church. In the East there was an empirical feeling attached to the local community, much more than an idea bearing upon *the* (universal) Church.[57] There was also a taste for freedom and a kind of individualism or particularism which called for free discussion and which should fit into a collegial or synodal regime.[58] In fact, the East was eventually to crystallize its canonical tradition along the lines of administrative autonomy of the local churches (as expressed by Canon 5 of Nicaea and Canon 8 of Ephesus) with only very grave matters to be brought before a council. Rome, on the other hand, was to tend more and more to intervene in the life of the churches, certainly for their welfare, to be sure—and was soon to insist upon considering that what she had judged was no longer a matter to be discussed, but to be carried out. The case of the two great councils, of Chalcedon and of Ephesus, where the Roman primacy was clearly established, is a significant example. At Ephesus the East, that is, Cyril and his followers, had passed judgment already before the arrival of the legates. But in Rome the matter was already considered judged by the letters of Celestine. When the legates arrived in Ephesus, Nestorius being already condemned and deposed, they called attention to the fact that the Council had been called together to carry out the decisions already made in Rome, and to adhere to the faith of the Head.[59] Very instructive for Chalcedon, especially if we compare it with the opposite tendency, noted previously with regard to Sardica, was the slight variation which is found between the two following texts. The first is that of the Papal legates to the Council, and the second that of Pope Leo I communicating the judgment to the Bishops of Gaul:

> For these reasons, Leo, the most holy and most blessed Archbishop of the great and older Rome, through us and *through this holy synod here assembled*, and in union with the thrice-blessed Peter the apostle who is worthy of all praise and is the stone and support of the Catholic Church and the foundation of the true faith, deprived Dioscorus of all episcopal dignity...[60]
>
> For these reasons the holy and most blessed Pope Leo, head of the universal Church, through us his legates, *with the agreement of this holy synod*, endowed with the dignity of the Apostle Peter...[61]

It is the same text, and yet there is a subtle difference between the Greek version and the Latin translation.

According to the law followed in the West and in ecclesiastical life, from the end of the Fourth Century onward, the Decretals—that is to say, the papal epistles replying authoritatively to some questions—take on more and more importance. We have already noted this date in conjunction with the Council of Constantinople (381), then with the reply of Damasus (382) and with a whole series of his immediate successors, as the crucial one when the East and the West began to drift apart ecclesiologically. It was also exactly the period when the Byzantine Church provided itself with a canonical institution corresponding to the Roman synods, the council of the Pope, whose judgments, once given, become imperative: the σύνοδος ἐνδημοῦσα or permanent synod. The institution began to function after the Council of 381, even though it did not officially receive its name of synod until the Council of Chalcedon.[62] Between 381 and 451, Constantinople extended its jurisdiction over the two "dioceses" of Asia Minor; Canons 9 and 17 of Chalcedon laid down the procedure for appeals to the Patriarchal See. The permanent synod became an ecclesiastical tribunal of empire; and this at the very time when Rome, for her part, was affirming her right of universal judgment.

But the creation of a properly so-called Oriental canonical tradition came long after this. Two great blocks entered into it: (1) the legislation of Justinian I, under whom the opposition of an Eastern tendency towards Monophysitism was particularly felt and, in the West, a sharper affirmation of the dual nature of Christ;[63] (2) the canons of the Quinisext Council (the Second Council of Trullo) of 692. At this council, canons were enacted which were not only based on the right of local churches to self-determination but in the very name of the Apostles—canons which in reality dated only from the Fourth and Fifth Century.[64] Pope Sergius refused his signature. In the subsequent quarrels between the East and Rome, at the time of Photius and of Cerularius in particular, and even today, a great portion of the grievance over rites, customs, and discipline that the Easterners were to put before Rome, would have their source in the canons of this Second Council of Trullo, which had assumed the force of law in the East but had not been recognized by Rome.[65] When, for example, the quarrel broke out in 905 over the fourth marriage of Emperor Leo VI, which was to be another stage in the alienation of the two churches, it was in the name of his own legislation and his canonical autonomy that the Patriarch of Constantinople was to resist a decision taken by Rome in the name of her own tradition.[66] The decisive estrangement, however, in matters of law, liturgy and customs dates from 692.[67] This is also the date of the Monothelite dispute, the Arab conquest, the growth of the Church in the Germanic lands, where the devotion to St. Peter was to flourish.

*The West—The Pope as Primate and arbiter for
the Universal Church.*

Quite soon, Rome became conscious of her power to
promulgate definitive decrees, valid in themselves, anywhere
in the world. Without doubt, testimonies to this could be
found from the time of, say, Pope Victor (189-199); but
we are not at present writing a history of the primacy. It is
certain that Rome, in her various contacts with the East,
has always held this position. Apparently it is also scarcely
debatable that the East, except for a few remarkable cases,
never willingly and unreservedly admitted that something
decided in the East by a synodal tribunal and according to
Eastern tradition, should be considered as not decided and
therefore subject to a decision from Rome which, once given,
would be irreversible and without appeal. The cause of the
Easterners opposing the Council of Sardica was doubtless
bad from a doctrinal point of view; but are we straining the
meaning of the motives advanced if we see in them an initial
protestation against the rejudging of a cause already judged
by a council in the East? [68] At the same time the Eastern
bishops who were partisans of Eusebius were reproaching
Pope Julius I for having supported Athanasius despite the
Council of Tyre where he had been judged and deposed. [69]
But Rome maintained her position, and that brilliantly, as
for instance at the Council of Ephesus where the behavior
and actions of the legates could not be more unambiguous. [70]
There is no lack of the most explicit declarations by the
popes. [71] And in the affair of Photius we shall soon find
the clash between the Roman "already-judged" and the Byzantine intention to follow the Eastern synodal procedure.

68

And yet, when the popes of the Fifth Century addressed themselves to the bishops of the East, they did not do so in the same tone and manner they adopted when addressing themselves to the bishops of Italy or even, more generally, to the bishops of the West. To the West, the popes spoke in the tone of the decretals; the East was treated as an associate.[72] Let us recall what was said above on the three zones of the papal *potestas*. The development was oriented towards a certain abolition of the lines of demarcation between these different zones. The papacy tended to govern all the churches as if they were within her metropolitan competence and, from the liturgical point of view as well as from the canonical and, apparently, from the dogmatic as well, to bring them in line with herself.[73] She succeeded in the West except, of course, in the countries affected by the Reformation—England being the particularly interesting case—but never in the East.

We may now note the principal stages of the centralizing movement in its beginnings: Nicholas I and the False Decretals[74] take us to the epoch of Photius, to Gregory VII and his powerful reform, and to the epoch of Cerularius.[75]

Photius and Cerularius: differences become formal opposition

The history of the events has been remarkably well recreated (or reestablished) by Catholic scholars; there are the works of Grumel and Jugie, of Amann and Dvornik (especially the latter) on the Patriarch Photius.[76] But this history has not been studied in the perspective of ecclesiological and canonical ideas, although this point of view is of prime importance. Throughout the history of the estrangement we have the feeling that each side took up its stand without clearly stating it, in the name of a theology of the Church, of her unity, of her regime, and of the conditions of her union.

Rome, especially under Nicholas I, acted in the conciousness of her primacy understood as *plenitudo potestatis;* she wished to impose upon Constantinople her point of view of an authority regulating everything in the Church, directly and definitively.[77]

Constantinople, on the other hand, whether represented by the Emperor or by Photius, or by other Eastern Patriarchs, acted as if power were exercised in the Church by the Pentarchy of the Patriarchs and by the Councils; as if that power were less a personal authority than a tradition preserved by the churches,[78] its exercise being controlled by the Councils, and in the intervals between Councils, by the fact of communion between the great sees which manifested itself particularly by the sending of synodal letters. This opposition of ideas was obvious at the Council that opened on October 5, 869.[79] The legates wanted only to execute a sentence already handed down by Rome, whereas the Byzantines wanted the Council to take up the question from the beginning, with an investigative hearing of the accused: this is evident in the reticence of the Eastern bishops and the suggestions or demands of the wily Emperor.

The human estrangement had reached its peak at the time of Photius,[80] who seriously increased the psychological tension and misunderstanding by transforming simple *differences* into *oppositions* by strenuous polemic.[81] Even after the reestablishment of union, both sides sank deeper into that "state of reciprocal ignorance" of which Jugie speaks. The general situation was favorable to Byzantium and unfavorable to Rome. At the end of the Tenth Century, the popes succeeded each other rapidly and were caught up in political and family intrigue, and this in the midst of anarchy and civil war. Between 896 and 1049, there was a succession of 43 popes, not one of whom has left a memory of a significant attempt at reconciliation with the East. In Byzantium, during the same time, the ecclesiology of the Patriarchs found definite expression entirely to the benefit of Constantinople,[82] and there was a strengthening of the intention to establish total independence. Historians admit[83] that the split had virtually occurred before Cerularius or from the beginning of the Eleventh Century, the time of Sergius II. No longer was word received in Rome from the East; when Peter of Antioch sent his synodal letter to Pope Leo IX, it was a matter for pleased astonishment. In 1025, the Patriarch Eustathius expressed to John XIX the desire that Constantinople might be independent and sovereign "in suo orbe."[84] Thus, Jugie has been able to write of the separation that took place in 1054: "Instead of speaking of a definitive schism, it would doubtless be more exact to say that at this date we are in the presence of the first abortive attempt at reunion."[85]

The part played by Cerularius was still the decisive one. Likewise decisive was the part played by the Roman legate, combative, stiff-necked Cardinal Humbert, whose bull of excommunication is a monument of unbelievable lack of understanding.[86] Rome was certainly too ruthless at a moment which, as events were to prove, happened to be crucial, even though we may to some extent dissociate her cause from that of her impetuous legate, since the Pope had been dead for several months when Cardinal Humbert placed the bull of excommunication on the altar of Santa Sophia. We might indeed even question the canonical validity of the gesture.[87] But Cerularius very decidedly wanted the rupture. He wanted complete independence for Constantinople, and he worked towards that end not only against the Pope but against the Emperor Constantine Monomacus, whose anti-Norman policy in Southern Italy called for an entente with the Pope.[88] Cerularius wanted anything but an entente with the Pope and did everything to make the breach a lasting one, if we discount a few of his overtures that were calculated to put the imponderables on his side and give him the appearance of being justified. We can even attribute to him the ambition to supplant both the Pope and the Emperor.[89] By his violent polemic he poisoned the atmosphere. Wrapped up in his Byzantine tradition just as Humbert was in the Roman tradition, Cerularius accused the Latins of heterodoxy on all the points of custom or discipline in which they did not agree with his own practices.[90]

Even so, we have to recognize here once more something other than a vulgar quarrel or an act of personal ambition. The "Oriental schism" can no more be explained by the ambition of Cerularius than the Reformation can be explained by Martin Luther's efforts to shake off the yoke of his religious vows. There were also two ecclesiological systems confronting each other. The legates declared to Cerularius, as they had formerly done at the Council of 869, that they had come "not to learn and discuss but to teach and convey their decisions to the Greeks."[91] Humbert was the man of the Gregorian reform, and in ecclesiology he held the most rigid views on pontifical power, as was presently to be seen in the famous *Dictatus Papae*, a kind of syllabus originating, it has recently been suggested, as a document responding to the conditions of union expressed by the Greeks, directed against the theory of the Pentarchy and setting forth the basic terms on which Rome would agree to resume union with the East.[92] It is not merely a polemical thesis proposed by that frenetic adversary of the papacy, Paolo Sarpi,[93] but rather an explanation admitted by many Byzantine scholars that the Gregorian reform movement contributed by its wilfully ruthless ways and by its ecclesiological tendencies to precipitate the breach.[94] At any rate, in the Twelfth and Thirteenth Centuries, Byzantium was to critizise the absolutism, the centralization, and the fiscal policies of the Roman Curia to which the necessary and grandiose reform of Gregory VII was, so to say, the preface.[95]

We have reached the culminating point: the schism has occurred. Our thesis on the progressive estrangement has reached the date of 1054 which, though far from being the date of a total alienation, is a fatal one, since it seems to mark one of the greatest misfortunes that have ever befallen Christianity.[96]

And now, what can be done, what can we conclude?

CHAPTER FIVE

CONCLUSION
THE LESSONS OF HISTORY

The present, which is given us for action, is illumined by the past; history provides us with experiences of the past which can prepare us for the future. We can therefore ask ourselves two questions: What is the balance sheet of history on the actual substance of the "Oriental schism?" What can we do that will contribute to bringing it to an end?

THE "SCHISM" LIES PRIMARILY IN THE ACCEPTANCE OF THE ESTRANGEMENT

From the earliest centuries, manifold "differences" between East and West about practically everything evolved in such divergent ways that soon an estrangement began to set in which was hardened by mistrust and mutual ignorance. This development was gradual and simultaneous on almost every point of difference.

At some periods, political questions dominated, at others ecclesiological questions came to the fore. But from the beginning to the end, the estrangement affected the whole situation, so that the different aspects that we have discerned and treated separately, must be reconstituted in a complex process as continuous as life itself. At times we have mentioned azymes, at others the *Filioque*; we have at times spoken of barbarism, and finally of papal monarchy. There were and still are many points of opposition, but in the long run there was *an* opposition, the opposition of an East and a West.

The separation became more marked by the fact that each of the two portions of Christendom withdrew behind the barrier of its own tradition and always judged the other from the point of view of that tradition. Following the breach of 1054, each side set up its particular tradition as an absolute; oppositions became fixed, with the result that every step taken towards union, only resulted in a greater separation.[1] Moreover, it must be recalled that the following century and a half was a period of great change in the West. In studying over a period of years our differences and the dialogue with our Orthodox friends, when we examined more closely the theological points that are the stumbling blocks, we saw that they crystallized in their present forms in the West particularly from the end of this Eleventh Century, in which the estrangement became a complete separation.[2] Many of these points have since been the subject of dogmatic definitions in the West which only increases the difficulty. A dogmatic definition is not merely a juridical fact, but it is a reality touching the conscience of the Church, implying a maturing of that consciousness and determining its content in a way which has profound repercussions. When a dogmatic definition is made without the participation of a portion of Christendom, an occasion for estrangement is created which may never be adjusted. We have a significant example of this in the case of the Armenians who, by force of circumstances, remained outside the Christological debates of the Fifth Century and the Council of Chalcedon, and thus became Monophysites.[3] Theological thought was amazingly active in the West from the Eleventh Century onward, but it was almost exclusively *Latin*, especially since Scholasticism soon entirely dominated it, and Scholasticism was an exclusively Western phenomenon. In fact, so thoroughly Western was it—and this is one of the remarkable constants of its history—that several attempts to introduce into Scholasticism the Greek point of view provoked a crisis.[4]

In any case, the ecclesiological difference that we pointed out, with regard to the ways of organizing the life of the Church, was strongly accentuated. In the very documents calculated to reestablish union, Innocent III speaks of decisions made by the Pope as completely binding in themselves, just as his predecessor Nicholas I, the legates of Hadrian II in 869, or Leo IX had done, in 1054.[5] Later on, at the time of the Conciliar Movement, the author of a treatise composed in 1406, is under no illusions when he flatly sets the Eastern law (wholly based on the canons of councils) towards which, in fact, his preferences inclined, in opposition to the law that was growing in the Latin Church, which rested on the inalterable decision of authority.[6] The elimination of Conciliarism on the very eve of the Council of Florence, then later, that of Gallicanism and Episcopalism, not to mention the tightening that took place during the Counter Reformation, inevitably resulted in a further sharpening of the difference in the way of conceiving the life of the Church.[7]

Quite frequently in this book, we have made the point that the estrangement has created further suspicion. We have even encountered the evil and vicious offspring of this suspicion which has generated the violent anti-Latinism that, more than once has cried: "Death rather than Rome! Rather the

turban of Islam than the mitre of Rome."[8] Now, it is well
known that, in accordance with one's feelings, one either
looks for and finds a basis of agreement, or, on the other
hand, tends to push differences into formal oppositions and
thus soon contrasts become contraries.[9] A mind entirely
set on resistance and opposition fundamentally does not *want*
union; it not only does not seek or see the means, it does
not even believe in the possibility of union and in fact does
not even want that possibility. Luther, in his time, upon
learning that a Reform Council was finally to be opened and
that it would no doubt accord the chalice to the laity, declared
that, in despite of the Council, he would establish communion
under only one species and would anathematize those who
would follow the Council.[10] Certain complaints, only too
often repeated by the Orthodox down the centuries, indicate
a complex of distrust and disdain which erects a mental barrier
and thus blocks the path to unity. On the other hand, we
have a quite remarkable example of what hearts really filled
with the spirit of unity can accomplish in the interpretation
of differences: it is to be found in the admirable letter which
Peter, Patriarch of Antioch, wrote to Cerularius shortly after
the events of July 1054; it is again to be found in the responses
made 35 years later, by Theophylactus, Archbishop of Bulgaria, in a letter to a cleric of Constantinople who had spoken
to him of the shortcomings of the Latins.[11]

"It is recounted," writes Tournier, "that when Im Grund
went to Nicholas de Flüe to tell him of the grave dissensions
of the Confederates and to ask for his advice, the blessed
Nicholas took his rope girdle, tied a knot in it and held it
out saying, 'Will you untie this knot?' Im Grund easily
did so. 'It is thus,' said Nicholas 'that we must untangle the

difficulties of mankind.' But when his interlocutor protested, saying that it was not as easy as that, Nicholas replied, 'You would not be able to untie this knot in the rope either, if we both pulled on each end, and that is always the way people try to untangle their difficulties.' " [12]

Now, in quoting this allegorical tale, as well as in the exposition that precedes it, we may perhaps have seemed to present Rome and Constantinople as two separate Churches, equal partners in a conflict in which each has committed wrongs obviously of the same degree of seriousness. And certainly all the wrongs have not been on one side: Humbert of Romans quite frankly admitted that in his admirable memoir for the Council of Lyons in 1274 which we have already cited.[13] He likewise even posed the question: "Why do we call the Greeks schismatics rather than the Latins?"[14] And he replied as follows:"It is because they are in rebellion against the Head." Both the question and the answer are of sufficient importance as to deserve a pause for detailed discussion. Recently, an Anglican posed fundamentally the same problem, not quite seriously, however,[15] but for lack of a solid ecclesiology and being a victim of the vague nominalism so widespread in England, perhaps he did not know how to reply to it. One can only reply if one has (1) an *organic* idea of the Church; and (2) an ecclesiology of the Universal Church.

The total Church is a unit and as such, has her own structure. The Church is not composed *uniquely* of local churches identical in worth, although the Church is this. Nor is each local church merely a *collectio fidelium*, made up solely of the individual faithful, identically situated in regard to the apostolic faith. "Illi sunt Ecclesia," says St. Cyprian, "plebs sacerdoti adunata et pastori suo grex adhaerens."[16] ("These make up the Church: a people united to its priesthood and a flock at one with its shepherd.")

In the Church there are simultaneously multitude and hierarchy, cells and a principle of unity: in short, it is an organism. In the *Acts of the Apostles* likewise, the Church is defined as the faithful who joined themselves to the Apostles and submitted to their rule.[17] And the Apostles themselves were not twelve individuals but "The Twelve"; they formed a body, a college; they were organically united. The congregation were "those with the Twelve"; the Eleven were "those with Peter."[18] Within the Church, there is an organic structure; all parts of it are the living stones of the edifice, some being the foundation stones. Or, to change the figure of speech, all members of the Church are members of a flock, some being shepherds, and all belong to the house of God, of which some are stewards.[19] But among the foundation stones, one apostle is the rock upon which the edifice is built (Matthew 16.18); and among the shepherds, one has received the universal charge of the flock (John, 21); among the stewards, there was one upon whom were first bestowed the keys which the others subsequently obtained with him. The comparison of Matthew 16.16-19, with Matthew, 18. 15-18, which is often made in the controversies between the Orthodox and Catholics is at this point very appropriate. There are *two* texts, the only two of the Gospels in which the word *ecclesia* is spoken by Jesus, and ecclesiology must honor *both* texts. One of the texts applies to the jurisdiction of the bishops in each local *ecclesia*, ·the other applies to the jurisdiction of Peter in the *ecclesia universalis*.

It should be understood that we make these brief remarks not so much to *prove* in a few lines a thesis which a large volume would scarcely suffice to establish, as to clarify and illustrate what we have to say. In the preceding pages we have seen how the East was mainly interested in local churches and the immediate experience acquired through living in them; how it paid little attention to the jurisdictional implications of the Church as a society centered, as it was, upon the mystical and sacramental aspects of ecclesiastical life: all reasons why the East has only poorly succeeded in realizing an ecclesiology of the Universal Church. But the Universal Church exists and, under God, possesses her structure as a Church Universal. If we say under God, we mean that it was instituted by Jesus Christ. But we do not mean to deny in expressing ourselves in this way, that history, circumstances, canonical determinations and other causes, all under providential guidance, have contributed greatly to the development of pontifical authority and to the modalities, of themselves contingent and variable, for its actual exercise. This fact was recognized more widely and more generously by the ancients, popes as well as theologians, than is customary today by Catholic apologetics, harried as it is by controversy.[20]

All this shows sufficiently well that, in the separation brought about by a long and general estrangement, the faults are not equal, even though they are shared. In a quarrel between a father and a son, the responsibilities are never equal. Authority may have its faults, but it can never be fundamentally at fault; we may rightly have reasons against it, but we are never right to go against it. Authority has its fundamental and intrinsic justification by its legitimate right, and by law. It is for this reason that we may say, speaking in all objectivity, that the Greeks rather than the Latins should be called schismatics. In the Oriental schism, which at this point we may write without the quotation marks, there are not merely two portions of Christianity which have drifted apart; there is an ensemble of local churches which separated themselves from the Apostolic See of Peter. This means that they are separated from the Center which exercises, with the primacy, the role of moderator of the Universal Church, of guide in her life, of criterion of her unity. This is also why—as we have never concealed, either from our Orthodox friends or from our Protestant friends—that union, while not representing an "absorption" in the odious sense of the word, can only be, from the point of view of ecclesiology, a reunion with the Apostolic See. This may be said in a few words, but these words are decisive, for ecclesiologically speaking, they qualify the whole historical process which we have traced in broad lines.

Still another remark is necessary if our account is to be entirely truthful, not so much from the point of view of ecclesiology, as from that of history. It is impossible to develop all the themes at once. Our theme has been that of "estrangement." To be entirely fair, we should also have noted at each stage the profound reality of what remains common to both portions and the valiant efforts expended on each side to maintain communion. All through this long history and continuing after 1054, there have been the realities of a shared Christian life and Church,[21] friendly acts,[22] concessions,[23] a pro-Rome party in Constantinople, a pro-Oriental party in Rome.[24] To collect and evaluate all these matters would require a separate study. But these efforts were not the ones which have prevailed in the course of history. Since 1054, no effort has succeeded in uniting the two parts of the Christian world in an enduring form and we are still faced with the fact that the living tissue of the Church, so tragically torn apart at that time, is still unmended.

THE TASKS THAT LIE AHEAD FOR THE ACHIEVEMENT OF UNION: PREPARATORY STUDIES, UNDERSTANDING AND MUTUAL CHARITY.

Much work has already been accomplished. For neither side, especially the Roman, has ever resigned itself fully to the separation.[25] Explanations have been exchanged, and some rather remarkable progress may be noted. This progress becomes clear if, for example, we compare the discussions on the subject of the *Filioque* at different periods of history. At the synod of Nicaea-Nymphaeum in 1234, neither party would cede a point, but maintained its position to the letter. At Florence, in 1438-1439, where the discussion was straight-forward and penetrating, it was limited by imperfect exegetical and patristic resources. Compare these two also with conferences on the same question held during the Nineteenth and Twentieth centuries,[26] and it will be seen that great progress has been made in the documentation and comprehension of each other's point of view; yet, this question was for a long time presented as the decisive and insurmountable reason for the separation.[27] The dispute has now reached the point where more than one Orthodox theologian has declared that the doctrinal question of the *Filioque* would not be an obstacle to the reestablishment of union.[28] Today the more commonly held view is that, fundamentally, there is but one decisive point of difference: the question of the primacy,[29] and, of course, the question of the infallibility of the Pope, which is intimately connected with the primacy but involves its own special difficulties.

Thus, to some extent the way has been cleared. Why should not more of this clearing-up be done, and on these very points which today seem to present an insurmountable obstacle? We can hope for much in this respect from historical studies. Batiffol sees "a great virtue of pacification and concord" emerging from them;[30] we would add: and of union in the truth.

As we have said, much work has been done; the attempts at reunion have multiplied in the course of the centuries,[31] and yet, despite some limited "successes" reunion has not taken place. Much work has been done, but the estrangement remains. We must therefore learn a lesson from these past failures for the future. Perhaps we should use the word in the singular, to give it greater weight: *the* failure to achieve reunion.

To begin with, there is the fact that all the negotiations, and indeed all the relations of any kind between the Greeks and the papacy, were for centuries closely linked with politics. On the one hand, the Emperor seemed to hold the key to everything: the Latins believed that with him the Church was won. But, the Emperor needed the Pope who was also a political power, to combat the Normans and to hold off the Turks. Especially after the Crusades, a politico-religious papacy successively considered two means of regaining the Greek Church through the *Basileus* without, however, neglecting the means of discussion and persuasion: military conquest and diplomatic negotiations, above all diplomatic negotiations.[32] Some reconciliations were thus arranged, some unions concluded. But oftentimes, nothing of this survived, except perhaps, a heightened distrust and the whole estrangement. The reason for this was, that apart from these diplomatic overtures, and on a much deeper level, "the vast world of the East continued to lead its life without worrying any more about Rome, and Rome continued to exist without caring whether or not it was understood and loved by the East."[33]

The Council of Florence, in regard to which the Orthodox seem to us to be excessively unjust, marked a considerable advance. Owing to the participation of learned theologians from the West and the East, it was, in fact, a great theological debate. Then came the fall of Constantinople, after which the problem caused by the political power of Constantinople was lessened. In modern times, the end of Czarism and the constitution of independent countries in Central and Balkan Europe, and along the Baltic after World War I have often been hailed as a promise that the political problem had, at long last, been finally eliminated.[34] Unfortunately, however, it still exists and has appeared in other forms: the dividing line, cutting the world into an Eastern World and a Western World, has, for a vast extent of Eastern lands, become an "East-West curtain," which places Greece and Constantinople politically on the side of the West; but even this does not make things any easier. The period of bargaining against a political background may be considered finished, but the period of the estrangement has not yet come to an end.

We may well ask the crucial question: has each side as yet done everything that needs to be done, in order to understand and to love, everything to make itself understood and loved?

The advances made to the East from the Catholic side in modern times, seem to be dominated by the sincere desire to *respect* the Eastern churches in their own *rites*. The documents promising the East respect and enjoining the Latins to this respect, have been extremely numerous, especially in the past century.[35] The papacy seems to have considered the

85

problem of reunion as that of a double and reciprocal recognition; the recognition by the papacy of the rights and canonical practices of the Orientals, their recognition of the traditional primacy of the Roman See. On the part of Rome, it would seem that everything could be summed up as fol_lows: We respect and shall respect your rites and your discipline; there is no reason why you should not come back to us.[36]

It seems to us that these conditions are fair, but only if they are taken with full seriousness and with all their deepest implications. Neither the rites nor the primacy can be reduced to a purely canonical and external question. We are dealing with extremely profound realities, varying though they be in importance, and coming to us from God by different paths. But on both sides there must be acceptance of things as they are: acceptance of the East as the East, acceptance of Rome and the West as the West and as Rome. This amounts to recognizing the inalterable conditions of unity which, providentially, are especially borne by Rome, and also recognizing the full diversity which, under God's Providence, is offered the Church under the species of the duality of an Eastern and a Western Christendom.

On the part of the East, there is need of an openmindedness towards what is irreversible in the development of the theological theory of the Church, and in the fact of the primacy: not necessarily the primacy in all the modalities it has been made to take on by history, or even in its present-day form, for a great portion of these elements are of relative and historical order; but a papacy in that minimal form compatible with a local ecclesiastical autonomy such as Photius acknowledged under Nicholas I, and the Bulgarians under Innocent III, and which Innocent IV still found the Greeks ready to accept.[37] This presupposes the successful completion of a vast amount of ecclesiological, biblical and historical work. On the part of the West and Rome, it all comes back to their accepting *in truth* the existence of an East, with its own mentality, its genius, its temperament, and its history, and the right it has to be known, accepted and loved for what it is. How good it is to be able to write with A. d'Avril, "We must not let the Orientals believe that they are tolerated, with their diversities, as an annoying necessity; no, the Catholic Church loves them for themselves, for what they are, and she would not want them to be otherwise."[38] This, of course, must be entirely true if it is to have real validity. It is easy enough to say: "Let the Orthodox realize that the return towards Rome does not imply the renunciation of any element of their legitimate tradition; but there is only one way for them to realize this, namely, that it be true; and the means for making it be true, is for us to believe in it, and to have no other desire in our hearts. The Orientals are never fooled as to our feelings for them; they appreciate every sign of *real* respect[39] and if such signs were to increase, the complex of distrust which shuts all the other doors, would surely vanish before long. For this, the scientific studies that have been pursued for several decades in the Catholic Church under the very powerful encouragement of the papacy, through the Assumptionist Fathers or the Pontifical Oriental Institute, are of inestimable value. Necessary as they are as preliminaries to a better understanding of things, these studies are, nonetheless, merely preliminaries. Even the rather general revival of interest in the Greek Patristic sources of Christian life and thought, as evidenced by Father Daniélou and the

French collection, *Sources Chrétiennes,* must be counted also on the level of preparations. We must hope that, thanks to all this and beyond all this, a true sympathy and a warm esteem for the Christian East will enter into the living tissue of Latin Catholicism.

Thus a general rapprochement is the indispensable preparation for a reunion. No doubt, one of the causes of the failure of past advances and efforts, was the lack of psychological preparation on *both sides.* A reunion should not merely be discussed and decreed. If the historical process of the schism was a gradual and general estrangement, and if in substance it consists in the acceptance of a situation of non-rapport, then the reunion, which should be the cure of the schism, can only be the result of a resumption of contacts full of esteem and sympathy—two words that really stand for charity. Adopting the expression of a German author we have cited before, we can say that there will be no "Wiedervereinigung" (reunion) without long, patient, intelligent and loving "Wiederbegegnung" (renewal of contact). The actual means are not hard to imagine: what the heart desires, the mind will invent. Before arguing on the points of divergency, and especially before seeking union by way of canonical or diplomatic dealings, a psychological and spiritual reconciliation must be sought and feelings of confidence, and of real sympathy, aroused. This can only be done by converting into actual fact to the highest degree, and, if it be necessary, emphasizing the mutual affinity of the two churches[40]—or, if needs be, by recreating it. We have borrowed the phrase "mutual affinity" from an Anglican writer, just as we have borrowed the word "estrangement" from the English, thus proving that we can learn from those with whom we often disagree.

The Churches of the East and the West have an affinity between them that goes much deeper than their estrangement. The Orthodox are well aware of it, and some of them, not the least eminent in their Church, have told us that in their ecumenical conferences they felt they were also speaking for the Catholic Church. The differences will tend to grow in the same measure that they are not respected; similarly, if they are recognized for what they are, the profound affinities between the Churches will assert themselves and the chance for reunion will be strengthened. At the same time, the serious reasons which contribute towards a favorable reconsideration or interpretation of the disputed questions will be freed from the burden of the distrust which prevents them from exerting all their force. In any case, no matter how efficacious the visible results, one worthwhile consequence will at least have been attained: the spirit of schism will no longer be able to claim a place in our hearts.

We repeat: dogmatically and canonically, the main factor in the Oriental schism is the refusal to submit to the primacy of the Roman See; actually and historically, the schism is the result of a gradual and general estrangement. Not that the schism is of itself the estrangement; rather the schism is the acceptance of the estrangement. The sin of schism is already committed in the heart when we behave as though we were not an integral part of the whole with others, *alter alterius membra* (Rom. 12.5). In this organic whole which is the Church, each local church not only realizes the mystical nature of the whole, mainly through the sacramental life, but is itself also *a part* of that whole, according to the plan of God which is to assemble all mankind into one Church and to represent, in the catholicity of that Church, the infinite riches of His gifts. If the Church is like a body, of which the East and the West are, we might say, the two sides, Rome is the visible head of the body, for the purpose of regulating its movements as a unity. To accept each other really means that each accept the other according to the role that each is to play in the total organism; it means that each one accepts the other as members of the same body, according to the vocation and function that is assigned to each part.

Depending upon the dogmatic and canonical reality of non-submission to, or acceptance of, the Head, the schism is made or abolished at a single blow. The actual acceptance of the estrangement, according to history, had begun long before the year 1054; but it has not been completed so long as there exist, here and there, people who do not share the feeling of estrangement. We contribute to the schism, even today, whenever we assume the attitudes of estrangement, or when we accept the results of many centuries of alienation; we continue it every time we commit, even today, acts analogous to those, positive or negative, which in the past made evident a lack of union. On the other hand, we contribute towards ending the schism and actually end it, to the extent that it exists in us, by every act or attitude of ours which rejects and weakens that estrangement. Every time we recognize the existence of the East, and the East recognizes the existence of Rome and the West, to that extent, the wound has been healed.

NOTES

NOTES TO CHAPTER ONE

1. Indeed, this idea is clearly stated in the second part of the very remarkable *Opus tripartitum* by Humbert of Romans, especially in chapters 11 and 12; the text is quoted in Brown, *Appendix ad fasciculum rerum expectandarum et fugiendarum* II (London 1690). Of the many modern historians who have expressed the idea, we list only a few: A. Michel, "Bestand eine Trennung der griechischen und römischen Kirche schon vor Kerullarios ?"*Zeitschrift f. Kirchengesch.* 42 (1922) 1–11; A. Baumstark, "Grundgegensätze morgenländischen und abendländischen Christentums," (typewritten ms, Rheine 1932); M. Jugie, *Le Schisme byzantin, Aperçu historique et doctrinal* (Paris 1941) (see for example p. 1, and 229–233); E. Amann, *Histoire de l'Eglise* (Fliche et Martin, 7, Paris 1940) 139; G. Every, *The Byzantine Patriarchate 451–1204* (London 1947) see especially p. 153f; C. A. Bouman, "Scheiding en hereniging in het perspectie der Historie," *Het christelijk Oosten en Hereniging*, Oct. 1952, 93–101; R. Mayne, "East and West in 1054", *Cambridge Hist. Journal* 2 (1953–1955) 134–148; cf. 136, where the author cites as agreeing on this subject, W. Holtzmann, B. Leib, E. Herman, G. Ostrogorsky, Prince D. Obolensky, A. Michel.

2. In the sense as specified by us: "Culpabilité et responsabilité collectives," *Vie intellectuelle* Mar. 1950, 259–284; April 1950, 387–407; cf. also *Vraie et fausse réforme dans l'Eglise* (Paris 1950) 579–596.

3. L. Duchesne, *The Churches Separated from Rome* (London 1907) 110, lists between the years 323 and 787 five great interruptions of communion between Constantinople and Rome, representing a total of 203 years. Jugie *Le schisme byz.* 9, counts between the years 337 and 843, 217 years of interruption divided into seven schisms.

4. For a certain number of these, see Every, *op. cit.* 165 and 168–69 (in the Twelfth Century), 186, 191 (At Mount Athos, after the Fourth Crusade); Jugie, *op. cit.* 234f; A. Palmieri, *Theologia dogmatica orthodoxa*

II *Prolegomena* (Florence 1913) 85 f. H. Rees, *The Catholic Church and Corporate Reunion. A Study of the Relations between East and West from the Schism of 1054 to the Council of Florence* (Westminster 1940); S. Runciman, *The Eastern Schism. A Study of the Papacy and the Eastern Churches during the XIth and the XIIth Centuries* (Oxford 1955), cites a great many such cases; Francis Dölger, in *Relazioni del X Congresso internazionale di Scienze Storiche*, III *Storia del Medioevo* (Florence 1955) 92 (until the Twelfth Century there was a Benedictine Monastery founded by Amalfitans on Mount Athos); 112 (relations with southern Italy and even with Monte Cassino, until the Twelfth Century); Raissa Bloch, "Verwandtschaftliche Beziehungen des sächsischen Adels zum russischen Fürstenhause im XI. Jahrhundert," *Festschrift, A. Brackmann* (Weimar 1931) 184–206 (marriages).

5. It would seem that this criterion was applied in determining which saints should be invoked during the prothesis of the Byzantine rite, in the Roman edition of the Liturgy of St. John Chrysostom (Grottaferrata 1940; brought out in 1941 by the Congregation for the Oriental Church); cf. A. Raes, S.J.,"La première édition romaine de la liturgie de S. Jean Chrysostome en staroslave," *Orientalia christ. period.* 7 (1941) 518–26 esp. 521 522.

6. The union was not rejected everywhere at once: it is probable that the union agreed upon at Florence was upheld in Jerusalem, and perhaps at Antioch, until 1534; the Archbishopric of Sinai remained Catholic until the Eighteenth Century. Cf. C. Korolevsky in *Stoudion* 17 (Feb. 1929) and in *Irénikon* (Nov. 1929) 646 n. 2. As for instances of communion we are especially referring to the *communicatio in sacris*. These were numerous until the Eighteenth Century and did not really cease to occur until after the middle of the Nineteenth Century. There is no doubt that a close examination of the archives of the Roman congregations concerned would produce an ample harvest. We refer the reader to but a few of the publications: A. Battandier, *Le cardinal J. B. Pitra* (Paris 1893) 374 f. 377 and esp. 435–38. Dom Pitra justifies the numerous cases to which he refers by the fact that, according to him, no official canonical act of the Oriental Churches had denounced the union of Florence; but he considers that this could no longer happen in view of the many acts of hostility towards the Catholic Church. Dom Pitra contributed to a stiffening

of the Roman attitude in these matters around 1860; cf. R. Aubert, *Le Pontificat de Pie IX*, (Paris 1952) 479-80. But that attitude is already seen soon after the rejection, by the East, of the union concluded at Florence (Palmieri, *op. cit.* 105). Numerous facts concerning the Fifteenth– to Eighteenth Centuries can be found in *Echos d'Orient*, 1934 and 1935 (esp. 1935, 350-367, on the Jesuit Missions to Naxos in the years 1627-1643); "L'Unité de l'Église," Sept. 1936; *Stoudion* 3 (1928) 75f; *Irénikon* 1926, 181 f; 1930, 270, no. 1; and 1936, 561 (Russia of the Fourteenth and Fifteenth Century).

7. Cf. A. Fortescue, *The Uniate Eastern Churches* (London 1923) 190; Every, *The Byz. Patr.* 154. The case of Russia merits a special study. After the schism of Cerularius, the Metropolitan Hilarion (1051-1072) and his successors George, John I, John II, Ephraim I and Nicholas I (1096-1106) remained in communion with Rome. As to the fidelity of the Kievan monks in the Eleventh and Twelfth Centuries, see J. Martynov, *Acta SS, Octobris X* 868f. D. Papebroch was no doubt too generous when he opined that the Russian Metropolitans were Catholic until 1520, but in criticizing his opinion, V. De Buck admits he is partially right (cf. *Acta SS. Octobris* XI, III and IV, sections 9-12).

8. Since our article "Schism," *Dictionnaire de théologie catholique* XIV col. 1286-1312 (1938), there has appeared Vol. II of the great work by Ch. Journet, *L'Eglise du Verbe incarné* (Paris 1951), which contains an extremely thorough elaboration of the Thomist theology of schism.

9. *Op. cit.* part 2, 14 (Brown, 218).

10. The excellent formula of Jugie, *op. cit.* 188, referring to the situation in the first half of the Eleventh Century.

11. C. Silva-Tarouca, *Fontes historiae ecclesiasticae*, II (Rome 1933) 7, n. 51.

12. W. de Vries, *Der christliche Osten in Geschichte und Gegenwart* (Würzburg 1951) 72 f.: "Eine langsame, immer weiter fortschreitende Entfremdung führte schliesslich zum Bruch zwischen Ost und West"; Ostrogorsky, *Geschichte des Byzantinischen Staates* (2nd ed. Munich 1952) 266; Dölger, *Byzanz und die europäische Staatenwelt* (Ettal 1953) 288.

NOTES TO CHAPTER TWO

1. Cf. A. Karatschow, "Die Entstehung der kaiserlichen Synodalgewalt unter Konstantin dem Grossen, ihre theologische Begründung und ihre kirchliche Rezeption," *Kirche und Kosmos (Orthodoxes und Evangelisches Christentum*, Studienheft No. 2) (Witten 1950) 137–152. The same subject is treated under the same heading in the same collection, 153–168 by E. Wolf from a less ideal point of view and constitutes a critique of the Catholic thesis as well as of the Orthodox view. In seeking a certain logic in the sequence of ideas, we evidently risk presenting historical moments that are really unlike, as being intrinsically similar. According to Ostrogorsky, "The Relations between Church and State in Byzantium," *Seminarium Kondakovianum* 4 (1931) 122–134 (in Russian, with German summary), there never was any caesaropapism in Byzantium. The history of Constantinople has been a history of the emancipation of the Church from the control of the State; in this history, two periods can be discerned: first, a survival of Roman paganism, in which the Emperor played a part in the Church, a state of things accepted in the West even by the popes, as well as in the East; next, from the Seventh Century onward, the birth in both the East and the West, of a new "medieval" ideology, setting forth the distinction between the spiritual and the temporal, the independence of the Church from the State. The iconoclast conflict responded to the reaction of the Emperor to this tendency; it was formulated, for example, by the *Epanagoge* of 879-886. This point of view seems to be more or less that of Byzantinists such as Dvornik (see *supra* No. 3); L. Bréhier, *Le monde byz.* II, *Les institutions de l'Empire byzantin*, 444, 461f. On the other hand, Dom Chr. Baur, "Die Anfänge des Cäsaropapismus," *Arch. f. kathol. Kirchenrecht* 3 (1931) 99-113, sees the beginning of caesaropapism in Constans: in effect, Constans set himself up as autonomous judge of dogmatic formulae, decided whether communion should be maintained or not, and had himself recognized even by the bishops (Synod of The Oak) as holding a sovereign position beyond the laws.

2. Am. Gasquet, *De l'autorité impériale en matière religieuse à Byzance* (Paris 1879).

3. Among others by F. Kattenbusch, *Lehrbuch der vergleichenden Confessionskunde* I (Freiburg i. Br. 1892) 374-83 (Excursus on the ecclesiastical signification of imperial dignity); L. Bréhier and P. Batiffol, *Les survivances du culte impérial romain. A propos des rites shintoïstes* (Paris 1920) esp. 36f; Dölger, "Rom in der Gedankenwelt der Byzantiner," *Zeitschr. f. Kirchengeschichte* 56 (1937) 1-42; O. Treitinger, quoted *infra*, n. 6; H. Berkhof, *De Kerk en de Keizer* (Amsterdam 1936; German translation Zollikon-Zürich 1947).; Dvornik, "Emperors, Popes and General Councils, *Dumbarton Oaks Papers*, 6 (1951) 4-23, emphasizes the normal character of this role of the emperor which the popes themselves have, on the whole, recognized. Also Dvornik, "Pope Gelasius and Emperor Anastasius I," *Byzant. Zeitschr.* 44 (1951) 111-116; his view has been criticized by Michel, "Der Kampf um das politische oder petrinische Prinzip der Kirchenführung," in *Das Konzil von Chalkedon, Geschichte und Gegenwart*, A. Grillmeier-H. Bacht (Würzburg 1953) 557-62. Michel shows here and on p. 524f. and 540f. that the Hellenistic formulas on the sacred character of kings did not have the same meaning and did not play the same part in Byzantium as in Rome (the West). The debate has not been settled. Cf. K. M. Setton, *The Christian Attitude towards the Emperor in the Fourth Century, especially as shown in Addresses to the Emperor* (New York 1941); a work criticized by Berkhof in *Vigiliae christ.* 2 (1948) 120 f. Berkhof considers that St. John Chrysostom limited himself to showing the duality of the powers or domains, while St. Ambrose affirms the subordination of the one to the other. F. Dölger, *Byzanz und die europ. Staatenw.* 142 n. 2; W. Ullmann, *The Growth of Papal Government in the Middle Ages* (London 1955) 33, n. 4; cf. 16-17 and all of part III of the Introduction, 31f.

4. Gasquet, *op. cit.* 56 (sermons) 221-64 (well-known result of the imperial heresies which provoked conflicts with the papacy); Bréhier, *Le monde byz. L'évol. de l'Humanité* II (Paris 1949) 432f.

5. The *Basileus* was not a mere layman, but a consecrated person having a quasi-sacerdotal dignity in the Church (entry into the sanctuary, the

rite of communion at the time of his coronation, etc.) and a quasi-episcopal function in the care of souls. In the Fifteenth Century even, Macarius of Ancyra was to say that the Emperor Manuel II, bishop like other bishops, except for the power to celebrate mass, was above other bishops in the care of souls. The references to the text and to the studies made on them are very numerous: besides those given in our *Jalons pour une théologie du laïcat* (Paris 1953) 299, n. 360 and 340, n. 78, see Am. Gasquet, *op. cit.* 38f. and esp. 44f. and 55; Batiffol, "Sur le titre de 'pontifex' des empereurs chrétiens des Vᵉ et VIᵉ siècles," *Bull. Soc. des Antiquaires de France* (1926) 222f; F. Cavallera, "La doctrine du Prince chrétien au Vᵉ siècle," *Bull. de Littér. ecclés.* (1937) 67f. 119f. 167f; R. Janin, "L'empereur dans l'Église byzantine," *Nouv. Rev. théol.*, 77 (1955) 49-60. The popes themselves often gave such titles to the emperors, and the sovereigns of the West followed in this matter those of Byzantium: cf. *Jalons, ibid.* and J. Hashagen, *Staat und Kirche vor der Reformation. Eine Untersuchung der vorreformatorischen Bedeutung des Laieneinflusses in der Kirche* (Essen 1931); K. Voigt, "Leo der Grosse und die 'Unfehlbarkeit' des oströmischen Kaisers," in *Zeitschr. f. Kirchengesch.* 47 (1928) 11-17.

6. "Ecumenical" is rather hard to translate in its Byzantine usages ("Ecumenical Council," "Ecumenical Patriarch"): cf. for example, Gasquet, *op. cit.* 113. We do not believe that we are mistaken in translating it by "Imperial" or "of the Empire," in the sense that German historians speak of the "Reichskirche," "Reichspatriarch," provided we do not forget the "unitarian" ideal of which we speak further on, according to which the vocation of the Empire was to express and realize upon the earth the unique reign of God (of Christ), by assembling all the οἰκου-μένη, all the inhabited earth, under the authority of the Emperor, representative of God. Cf. Treitinger, *Die oströmische Kaiser- und Reichs-idee nach ihrer Gestaltung im höfischen Zeremonieli* (Jena 1938) 164-66. In the sense of "Ecumenical" = "of Empire," see R. Devreesse, "Le cin-quième concile et l'œcuménicité byzantine," *Miscellanea G. Mercati* III (Rome 1946) 1-15. One might also at times translate the word by "pa-triarchical" for example: the direction of the Patriarchical School fell to the "Ecumenical Professor," but no doubt in the sense of principal or universal professor; cf. Bréhier, *Le monde byz.* III, *La civilization byzan-*

tine, 493. As may be seen, the expression was rather vague, connoting without great precision an idea of universality; consequently, when combined in the title "ecumenical patriarch" (cf. Ch. IV n. 26) lending itself to expressing the idea of a supreme dignity exclusive of submission to the primacy of the pope.

7. This point seems to us well treated in Gasquet, 117f. Cf. the very subtle indications given by J. Gaudemet, "Droit romain et droit canonique en Occident aux IVᵉ et Vᵉ siècles," *Actes du Congrès de Droit canonique*... April 1947 (Paris 1950) 254–67, esp. 262: "Constituting themselves the auxiliaries of Christianity, the Christian Emperors rendered canon law binding as civil law. Hence, the Church herself did not have to formulate her law. She simply indicated the measure she wished and solicited it from the Emperor..." The author cites relevant examples and refers the reader to W. K. Boyd, *The Ecclesiastical Edicts of the Theodosian Code* (1905) 264; he specifies his thought by challenging the too systematic thesis of Hinschius, according to which, from Constantine onward, ecclesiastical law was *ipso facto* and totally state law, *jus publicum*.

8. Ἀλλ' ὑμεῖς μὲν τῶν εἴσω τῆς Ἐκκλησίας, ἐγὼ δὲ τῶν ἐκτὸς ὑπὸ Θεοῦ καθεσταμένος ἐπίσκοπος ἄν εἴην : Eusebius, *Vita Constantini* IV 24. The exact meaning of this text is still being debated. Dvornik, in the study cited n. 3 *supra* (sep. prtg. p. 12), who stresses the normal character of the situation, sees in it a corrective gloss of Eusebius, aimed at reducing the Emperor from the rank of Apostle to that of Bishop. W. Seston, "Constantine as a Bishop," *The Journal of Roman Studies* (Papers presented to N. H. Baynes) 37 (1947) 127-31, does not interpret it in the sense of τὰ ἐκτός, but in the sense of οἱ ἐκτός, that is, in the sense of propagator of the Gospels to the pagans: as in E. Th. Babut, "Évêque du dehors," *Revue critique* 68 (1909), 362-64; J. Palanque, *Histoire de l'Église* (Fliche et Martin, 3) 63 and Bréhier, and again Janin, *Nouv. Rev. théol.* 77 (1955) 50, n. 1 and very recently J. Straub, *Studia Patristica* ed. K. Aland and F. L. Cross (T. U. 64), (Berlin 1957). This seems to us very debatable as it does to V. Laurent in his review of Seston's article in the *Rev. des ét. byz.* 6 (1948) 115-16. We believe it concerns the exterior life *of the Church*: her defense, her organization, her material means, her

policy and also the exercise of juridical sanctions. Cf. Gasquet, *op. cit.* 48, 117f., 176f.

9. E. Miklosich and J. Müller, *Acta et diplomata graeca medii aevi sacra et profana*, 6 vols (Vienna 1860-1890) II 9, cited by Laurent, *Rev. ét. byz.* 6 (1948) 114; and *id.* "Les droits de l'Empereur en matière ecclésiastique: L'accord de 1380-82," *ibid.* 13 (1955) 6-20.

10. A contemporary Orthodox writer advances the same idea: A. Schmemann, "La théocratie byzantine et l'Église orthodoxe," *Dieu Vivant* 25 (1953/4) 35-53, esp. 45.

11. *Essai sur la théologie mystique de l'Église d'Orient* (Paris 1944) 172. May be useful compared with Palmieri, *Theologia dogm. orthod.* I 757f. Note that the strongest formulas on the power of the Emperor in religious matters are to be found among the great Canonists Balsamon and Demetrius Chomatenus.

12. See our prefatory note in the posthumous volume of A. Gratieux, *Le mouvement slavophile à la veille de la Révolution: Dimitri Al. Khomiakov* (Paris 1953).

13. T. G. Jalland, *The Church and the Papacy* (London 1944). In *Blackfriars* (Feb. 1945) 56-57, Dvornik criticized Jalland's way of presenting the role of the Emperor in 'a "caesaropapist" light. See our review in *Rev. des Sc. phil. et théol.* (1947) 282-87. Cf. the study by Michel cited *supra*, no. 3.

14. Of course we cannot here expound or even summarize this entire history; as we have said, the estrangement which fosters the "Oriental schism" is co-extensive with the history of the Church herself. However, in spite of everything, we would like to mention here a few of the events which Jalland sees as so many occasions or episodes of the ecclesiological conflict between the Church of Empire and papal Rome: (a) the 6th Canon of Nicaea (211f.); (b) the summoning of the Eusebians to Rome by Pope Julius, to present their accusations against Athanasius, the pope being aware that Eusebius of Nicomedia was by way of substituting the

dogma of the Emperor as law for the apostolic tradition (213-18); (c) the testimony of the Council of Sardica, so categorical that the confessional adversaries of Rome denied the authenticity of its Canons or at least of the final clause; yet, says Jalland, when we examine the list of signatories of the address to Pope Julius, we begin to think that this appeal issued from men having the feeling that an ecumenical organ was needed by the Church, that Rome was that organ, and that disjoined from her, one fell into subjection to the Imperial power (219-23); (d) the struggle between Constantius, and autocratic Emperor, and Pope Liberius, a struggle which represented that of two conceptions of the source of dogmatic truth in the Church, in as much as the "fall" of Liberius represented a momentary defeat of the apostolic tradition by the dogma of Caesar (224f.); (e) the rescript of Gratian and the edict of Theodosius, both of them in line with Sardica, but of short-lived success (246-49); (f) the Roman document dating back to Pope Damasus, in which is formulated with great clarity the point of view of Rome, according to the apostolic tradition (255-57); (g) the appeal to Damasus by Timothy of Berytus and the terms in which Damasus replied (258); or (h) in view of the caesaroapism of Theodosius, the promulgation by Pope Siricius of the "First Decretal," a juridical instrument adapted to the situation canonically established at Sardica according to which the Roman See is the universal arbiter of the life of the Church within the framework of the Christianized Empire (265-72); or again, from the same Siricius the claim, against Theodosius II, of a primacy of the Church of Rome which, in the body of the Church, is like the head in relation to the members (273-77) and yet again (i), under St. Leo, the affair of the 28th Canon of Chalcedon; or (j) the protestation of Felix III against the pretention of Constantinople, the city of the Emperor, to be the See of the "ecumenical patriarch"; and, in the face of the *Henoticon*, the dogmatic decree of the Emperor, the resistance of the same Felix III and the deposition by him of Acacius of Constantinople; and Gelasius I carrying this affair one step further; then (k) the theology of the resistance of the Studite monks, partisans at Constantinople of the Roman position, turning towards Rome in order to free themselves of the imperial tutelage; and finally, (l) there is the action of Nicholas I, the contemporary and in some respects antagonist of Photius, loudly claiming for the Bishop of Rome the canonical prerogative of the ecumenical authority—for example, the right to convoke the Synods; cf. Gasquet, *op. cit.* 149, 181-82). Thus the popes gradually came to regain the prerogatives involving a role of direction or supreme arbitration in the Church; the privilege of sending the Pallium (Gasquet, *op. cit.* 183f.), and to give the Councils their legitimacy and value (Wolf, [cited *supra*, n. 1]162f.).

15. *Op. cit.* 8-11, 18f. Dvornik, *National Churches and the Church Universal* (Westminster 1944), has likewise insisted on the fact that in the East national churches were organized quite early, having their respective liturgical languages and that these churches were sometimes within the Roman Empire, sometimes outside it (Persia, Armenia, Abyssinia). In the West, before the conversion of the peoples to Christianity, Rome had imposed her order, language and often her worship. This fact is also to be found in Bardy, cited *infra*, ch. IV, n. 1.

16. An interesting piece of evidence of the idea of a Church of Empire: in 1393, the Grand Duke of Moscovy, upon having had the diptychs bearing the name of the *Basileus* abolished, declared: "We have a Church, we no longer have an Emperor"; to which the Patriarch of Constantinople, Antonius IV, replied: "It is impossible to have the Church without having the Emperor." (Miklosich and Müller, *Acta et diplomata...* II 191;) and cf. Bréhier, *Le monde byz.* II 431; and on the episode, the article by M. de Taube, "A propos de 'Moscou Troisième Rome'," *Russie et chrétienté* (1948, 3/4) 24, n. 7.

17. Cf. Baumstark, "Grundgegensätze..." 18.

18. Cf. for what follows, Baumstark, *op. cit.* Sect. 4, 18f. and ch· III, 3. It is instructive to compare with this the Orthodox accounts, such as those of S. Zankov, *Die Orthodoxe Kirche des Ostens in ökumenischer Sicht* (Zurich 1946) 72f. or Schmemann, "'Unity', 'Division,' 'Reunion', in the Light of Orthodox Ecclesiology," Θεολογία 22 (Athens 1951) 242-54. See also C. Swietlinski, *La conception sociologique de l'oecumenicité dans la pensée religieuse russe contemporaine,* (Paris 1938). Similarly, from the point of view of the diversity which appears even in the apostolic times, we recall the conclusions of J. Olson, "L'évêque dans

les communautés primitives..." *Unam Sanctam*, 21 (Paris 1951) on a Pauline tradition (stressing the existence of a Universal Church) flourishing in Rome, and a Johannine tradition (stressing the existence of local communities, each one with its bishop) flourishing in the East.

19. Cf. *infra* Kattenbusch, *Lehrbuch d. vgl. Confessionsk.* I. 231-35. Notice, however, the phrase, "Preserve the Plenitude (τὸ πλήρωμα) of thy Church" in the prayer that precedes the final benediction in the liturgy of St. John Chrysostom.

20. S. L. Greenslade often stresses this fact in his *Schism in the Early Church* (London 1953).

21. In all the works concerning the Empire and the Byzantine Church. See particularly Dölger, "Rom in der Gedankenwelt der Byzantiner," *Zeitschr. f. Kirchengesch.* 56 (1937) 1-42 (a wealth of bibliographical information); W. Hammer, "The Concept of the New or Second Rome in the Middle Ages," *Speculum* 19 (1944) 50-62 (the idea of "Second Rome" was applied, even in the West, to towns where the Imperial court sojourned; Aix-la-Chapelle, Trèves, Milan, Reims, Tournai, Pavia, even Bordeaux). See also the numerous studies devoted to the theme of "Moscow, Third Rome," particularly M. Schraeder, *Moskau, das dritte Rome* (Hamburg 1929); H. Rahner, *Vom Ersten bis zum Dritten Rom* (Innsbruck 1949); de Taube, "A propos de Moscou, 'Troisième Rome'" *Russie et Chrétienté* (1948, 3/4), 17-24, taking account of a Russian study by N. Tchaev, "'Moscou, troisième Rome' dans la pratique politique du gouvernement russe du XVIᵉ siècle," *Istoriceskie Zapiski*, 17 (Moscow 1945) 3-23; W. K. Medlin, *Moscow and East Rome, a Political Study of the relations of Church and State in Moscovite Russia* (Geneva 1952).

22. Bréhier, *Le monde byz.* II 1f.; as is known, Montesquieu takes this point of view in *De la grandeur et de la decadence des Romains*. See also, particularly, the publications of J. B. Bury.

23. Cf. Dölger, *art. cit.* (*supra*, n. 21) 7f.; he shows that the Byzantines even claimed a monopoly on the title of "Romans."

24. Cf. Dölger, 31-34; this idea of the transfer of the primacy first appears in the monophysite John Philoponus in the Sixth Century, but not linked with the *Donatio Constantini* (31, n. 54), which later on was used to bolster it (36, n. 64).

25. Dölger, 13.

26. Dölger, 33f.

27. Cf. numbers 11, 12 14 and 16. Text in Karl Mirbt, *Quellen zur Geschichte des Papsttums und des römischen Katholizismus* (Tübingen 1934) n. 228.

28. Dölger, 36f.

29. E. Peterson, *Der Monotheismus als politisches Problem* (Leipzig 1935), reprinted in *Theologische Traktate* (Munich 1951) 49-147. See also *Relazioni del Congresso internazionale di Scienze Storiche*, II *Storia dell' Antichità* (Florence 1955) "*La Monarchie hellenistique*": A. Heuss, "*Ursprung und Idee*," 201-13; A. Aymard, *L'Institution monarchique*, 215-34.

30. Eusebius in *Laus Constantini* (Ed. Heikel, GCS 7, 195-295, Leipzig 1902). On this political theology of Eusebius and Constantine, cf. E. Schwartz, *Constantin und die christliche Kirche* 2nd ed. (Leipzig 1913); J. M. Pfattische, "Die Kirche in den Schriften Konstantins d. Grossen," *Histor.-Polit. Blätter*, 151 (1913) (754-70; F. E. Cranz, "Kingdom and polity in Eusebius of Caesarea," *Harvard Theol. Rev.* 45 (1952) 47-66 (bibliogr.); Dölger, *Antike und Christentum*, 3 (1932) 128-31, and *Byzanz u. europ. Staatenwelt*, 141; Ullmann, *The Growth...* 17, n. 4, and an overall history of Constantinople and Rome from the viewpoint of the unitary world idea, either for the benefit of the Empire and the Byzantine patriarchate or for the benefit of the papacy is found in K. Jantere, *Die römische Weltreichsidee und die Entstehung der weltlichen Macht des Papstes* (Turku 1936). For the rather considerable influence of Eusebius in orienting the themes of practical ecclesiology in Greek thought, see J. Ludwig, "Die Primatworte Mt. 16, 18-19 in der altkirchlichen Exegese," *Neutestl. Abhdlg.* XIX, 4 (Münster 1952) 45-47.

31. Cf. Gasquet, *De l'autorité impériale...*; Bréhier, *Le monde byz.* II 4; *Les survivances du culte impérial romain*, 47; Dölger, *art. cit.* n. 21, *supra.*

32. Here we find a point in ecclesiology which has already been touched upon and which seems important to us. In the East rather than in the West, the translation of the visible and terrestrial expression has been accomplished by the State. On the plane of the Church and the exterior Christian life, there has reigned, so it seems to us, a dialectic of the *celestial* life manifesting itself through grace in human sin and corruption. A Church which should have the form of a unique visible society is an ideal of the Catholic Church, if it is not carried to extremes, as in the famous pages of St. Robert Bellarmine (*De Eccle. Militante* III, c. 2), which lack a sense of eschatology and the corresponding dialectic.

33. L. Genicot, *Les lignes de faîte du moyen âge* (Tournai-Paris 1951), 21.

34. Pope Gregory II († 831) wrote to the Emperor Leo III: "Universus Occidens principi apostolorum fructus fidei profert ... quem omnia regna Occidentis tamquam Deum in terra colunt. Nos viam ingredimur in extremas Occidentis regiones versus illos qui sanctum baptisma efflagitant. Qua de causa nos ad viam, Dei benignitate, accingimus..." Cf. E. Caspar, "Gregor II und der Bilderstreit," *Zeitschr. f. Kirchengesch.* 52 (1933) 29-89; cf. Michel, art. in *Chalkedon* II 539. (n. 3, *supra.*)

35. Innumerable events support this statement. Thus, for example, Hugh Capet, even at that late date, made efforts to find a bride of imperial blood for his son Robert; cf. A. A. Vasiliev, *Dumbarton Oaks Papers* 6 (1951) 226-251. The *Basileis* jealously reserved for themselves the title of Emperor: the "Barbarian" princes were only ῥῆγες. On the conflicts of titles, in which something other than semantics is involved, see Jugie, *Le Schisme byz...*, 30, 158, n. 3 (Nicephorus Phocas); Bréhier, *Monde byz.* II 348-52.

36. Cf. Amann, *Histoire de l'Église* (Fliche et Martin 8), 59; other examples may be seen in Bréhier, *op. cit.* 52.

37. H. Pirenne, *Mohammed and Charlemagne* (New York 1955).

38. See for example, Every, *The Byz. Patriarchate*, 451-1204 which s not cited by Pirenne.

39. General criticism: aside from reviews (see *Speculum*, 23 [1948] 165, n. 1): H. Laurent, "Les travaux de M. H. Pirenne," in *Byzantion* 7 (1932) 495-509; M. Bloch, "La dernière œuvre d'Henri Pirenne," *Annales* 10 (1938) 325-30; L. Lambrecht, "Les thèses de Henri Pirenne," *ibid.* 14 (1939) 513-36; D. C. Dennett, "Pirenne and Muhammad," *Speculum* 23 (1948) 165-90; Genicot, *op. cit.* 25f.; H. Aubin, "Die Frage nach der Scheide zwischen Altertum und Mittelalter," *Histor. Zeitschr.* 173 (1951) 245-63; we know only the title of A. Riising, "The Fate of Henri Pirenne's Theses on the Consequences of the Islamic Expansion," *Classica et Mediaevalia* 13 (Copenhagen 1952) 87-130; Dölger, *Byz. u. d. europ. Staatenwelt*, 359f, n. 170 (ref.) 368f.; Edw. Perroy, "Encore Mahomet et Charlemagne," in *Rev. histor.* 212 (1943) 232-38. Theories based on the other factors have been given by Genicot, "Aux origines de la civilisation occidentale: Nord et Sud de la Gaule," *Miscellanea historica L. Van der Essen* (Louvain 1947) 81-93. Criticism of this theory on the grounds of the economic data brought forward have been expressed by E. Sable, "L'importation des tissus orientaux en Europe occidentale au haut moyen âge (IXᵉ et XIᵉ s.)" *Rev. belge de Philologie et d'hist.* 14 (1935) 811f. and 1261f.; F. L. Ganshof, "Notes sur les ports de Provence du VIIIᵉ au IXᵉ siècle." *Annales, Économies, sociétés, civilisations*, 2 (1947) 143-60; R. Dochard, "Au temps de Charlemagne et des Normands: ce qu'on vendait et comment on vendait dans le bassin parisien," *ibid.* 266-80.

40. Cf. Jugie, *Le schisme byz.* 234, n. 2; cf. *infra*, ch. IV, n. 12. Another consequence of the Mohammedan conquest was that, by suppressing the Churches of Africa, it destroyed a Christianity which, while being Western and Latin, had and maintained a relative autonomy in relation to Rome. Cf. F. Heiler, *Altkirchliche Autonomie und päpstlicher Zentralismus* (Munich 1941). Thus disappeared the sole resistance to a total Roman ascendancy in the West. Islam favored the constitution of *two* "primacies," the one functioning in the Christian East, the other in the West,

41. Bréhier, *Le monde byz.* II, 456f.

42. Cf. P.-G. Scolardi, *Au service de Rome et de Moscou au XVIIe siècle, Krijanich, méssager de l'unité des chrétiens et père du panslavisme* (Paris 1947). This study is very well worth reading.

43. For example, the writings of Nicolas Jakovlevic Danilevskij († 1885): cited in B. Schultze, *Russische Denker: Ihre Stellung zu Christus, Kirche, und Papsttum* (Vienna 1950) 106.

44. *Tractatus super Quatuor Evangelia* (ed. E. Buonaiuti, Rome 1930) 106, note 280.

45. *Opus tripartitum*, pars 3, c. 18; ed. cited *supra*, ch. I. n. 1.

46. Aside from our usual authors, this point is well explained in G. B. Howard, *The Schism between the Oriental and Western Churches, with Special Reference to the Addition of the Filioque to the Creed* (London 1892) 20f. H. Scott, *The Eastern Churches and the Papacy* (London 1929) 310; Dölger, *Byz. u. d. europ. Staatenwelt*, 286f. On the problems of civil and canon law arising from the duality of emperors, cf. W. Ohnsorge, *Das Zweikaiserproblem im frühen Mittelalter* (Berlin 1947); P. Koschaker, *Europa und das Römische Recht* (Munich 1947); A. M. Stickler, *Sacerdotium et Regnum nei Decretisti e Primi Decretalisti* (Turin 1953) 18f., 25.

47. The history of the epoch of Clovis well illustrates all this. In becoming Catholic in the West where Roman civilization and religion were practically overwhelmed by the Arian barbarians, Clovis aimed there at becoming a protector who would "henceforth render useless appeals to the Emperor of Byzantium." de Labriolle, *Histoire de l'Église* (Fliche et Martin) 4, 395. Byzantium recognized the victory of Clovis by conferring upon him the title of consul, a kind of fiction by which the fact became stamped with the approval of the Empire. But Byzantium again intervened in Spain against the Arianism of the middle of the Sixth Century.

48. After Charlemagne, the Emperors of Constantinople were careful to call themselves "Basileus of the Romans" (Dölger, *art. cit.* 10);

Michael II, Balbus, (820-29) writing to Louis the Pious, thus pens his address: "To the glorious King of the Franks and the Lombards, their so-called Emperor," Jugie, *Le schisme byz.*, 30, who cites some other instances.

49. J. de Pange, *Le Roi chrétien* (Paris 1949) 167. Compare Fustel de Coulanges: "The coronation of Charlemagne was, on the part of the Pope, a breach with Constantinople." *Histoire des Institutions politiques*, 6, *Les transformations*. (Paris 1892) 312.

50. See texts and references in Gierke, *Political Theories of the Middle Age*, trl. F. W. Maitland (Cambridge 1900) 126, n. 55. S. Mochi Onory, *Fonti canonistiche dell'idea moderna dello Stato* (Milan 1951) 233, 244, 264f. (one sole emperor in the *Orbis*); 165 (Huguccio: the Emperor of Constantinople no longer legitimate), 237 (one sole Emperor, but the Empire had been handed over to the Germans).

51. Thus Laurentius Hispanus, Johannes Teutonicus; cf. Mochi Onory, *op. cit.* 225, n. 3.

52. Thus Ricardus Anglicus, cited by Mochi Onory, *op. cit.* 267. The *Basileus* was usually treated as Emperor by the popes: by Gregory VII, and by Innocent III.

53. Even the election of Count Baldwin of Flanders as Latin Emperor of Constantinople in 1204 in effect pays homage to the permanence of the Byzantine Empire.

54. Fleury, *Hist. ecclesiast.* X 646-47. Cf. Palmieri, article on *Filioque* DTC V, 2, col. 2321.

55. Cf. Palmieri, *Theol. dogmat. orthod.* II 75-87. Jugie, *Schisme byz.* Ch. 5 and 6.

56. On the Crusades, aside from the general histories, see the works of the Orientalists and Byzantinists: R. Grousset, L. Bréhier, *L'Église et l'Orient au moyen age. Les Croisades* 2nd ed. (Paris 1907). For the history of the Crusades as a whole, from the viewpoint of gradual alienation

of the East and the West, see Howard, *The Schism between the Oriental and Western Churches...*, 38f. Of the lamentable effects of the Fourth Crusade upon the relations between Greeks and Latins see. W. Norden, *Der vierte Kreuzzug im Rahmen der Beziehungen des Abendlandes zu Byzanz* (Berlin 1898), and the volume cited *infra*, Chapter V, n. 32. A. Luchaire, *Innocent III: la question d'Orient* (Paris 1907); Palmieri, *op. cit.* 36-52, gives the bibliography of the whole question up to 1913, and has written the definitive history of the controversy. See also A. Frolow, "La déviation de la IVe Croisade vers Constantinople. Problème d'Histoire et de Doctrine," *Rev. Hist. des religions* 145 (1954) 168-87; 146 (1954) 194-219. On the part played by Venice and Amalfi, aside from various monographs, cf. H. F. Brown and W. Miller, in Vol. IV of *Cambridge Medieval History*, chapters 13 and 15 respectively. S. Runciman, *The Eastern Schism, A Study of the Papacy and the Eastern Churches during the XIth and the XIIth Centuries* (Oxford 1955). Following the documents, Runciman shows that the breach of 1054 was not really felt on either side as a definitive alienation of the Greek world from the Catholic Church of Rome. What caused the final break and irreparable hostility between the two portions of Christendom were oppositions of political interests and then the Crusades with their consequences of Latinisation. See also P. Lemerle, "Byzance et la Croisade," *Relazioni del X Congresso int. di Scien. Stor.* III *Storia del Medioevo* 595-620.

57. Cf. 3 *Kings*, 12. 24 and 2 *Paralip.* 11.4.

58. *Epist.* CXXVI, Petro legato: PL 215, 701. Besides Luchaire, see for the facts the review *Stoudion* (Feb. 1949) 27f. in note; for the ideas, see P. Villey, "La Croisade, Essai sur la formation d'une théorie juridique," *L'Église et l'État au Moyen âge*, 6 (Paris 1942) 228f.

59. Cf. C. Korolevski, "Le passage au rit oriental," *Irénikon* 6 (1929) 457-87, 477.

60. Bréhier, *Monde byz.* II 458, gives a very rich documentation of the Latinisation in different studies of Korolevski (numerous articles in *Stoudion* 1922-1929) a series of articles on "Le clergé occidental et l'apostolat dans l'Orient asiatique et gréco-slave," *Rev. apologét.*, (15 Nov.-15

Feb. 1923) a separate printing; a brochure on *L'Uniatisme: Irénikon coll.* 1927, n. 5–6); the articles of E. Michaud, "Études sur la latinisation de l'Orient," *Rev. intern. de théol.* 3 (1895) 217–42, 488–504 673–89, and 4 (1896) 108–29; this study concerns the Seventeenth and Eighteenth Centuries and is the work of an Old-Catholic; R. L. Wolff, "The organization of the Latin Patriarchate of Constantinople," *Traditio* 6 (1948), 33–60; E. A. R. Brown, "The Cistercians in the Latin Empire of Constantinople and Greece, 1204–1276," *Traditio* 14 (1958) 62–120; and finally H. L. Hoffman, "De Benedicti XIV latinisationibus in Const. 'Etsi pastoralis' et 'Inter multa'," *Ephem. Juris canon.* 4 (1948) 9–54.

61. Even Anselm of Havelberg, a broad-minded man, who spoke Greek, saw a sign of schism in the different way of celebrating the Holy Eucharist in the East (*Dial.* III 12, PL 188. 1225c). But it must be noted that the West has generally recognized the legitimacy of this celebration: thus Gregory VII, *Reg.* VIII, 1; ed. Caspar, 313, St. Anselm, *Epist. de sacrif. azymi et fermentati* and *Epist. de sacram. Eccl.* n. 1; *Opera*, ed. F. S. Schmitt, II 233, 240; Innocent III, cf. H. Tillmann, *Papst Innocenz III* (Bonn 1954) 216–17.

62. A few significant documents of Innocent III may be cited: Letter *Cum venisset* to the Archbishop of the Bulgarians, Feb. 25, 1204, P. Th. Haluscynsky, ed.; *Acta Innocentii III* (*Pont. Comm. ad redig. Cod. iur. canon. orient.*), *Fontes*, Ser. III, vol. II, Romae 1944 n. 52, 258f; Letters *Ex parte tua* of August 2, 1204, PL 215.407, *Fontes*, n. 61, 271; *Ex parte tua* of March 8, 1208, PL 1353; *Fontes* n. 109, 341. Compare for the role of monastic consecration, Letter *Super episcoporum* of October 4, 1208. PL 1468, *Fontes* n. 120, 352. It is important to note that here reordinations are not involved and that the validity of Greek orders is not questioned. But reunion or plenary reintegration into the Church is conceived as entailing the observance of Latin (Roman) practices. See also the bull *Quia divinae sapientiae* of 1215, taken up again in 1257 by Alexander IV.

63. The Greeks showed an equal inflexibility. See, for the azymes, Mansi, XXIII, 298; for the Procession of the Holy Spirit, 305. On the synod of Nymphaeum in 1234, cf. B. Palazzo, "Historique d'une dis-

cussion sur la Procession du Saint-Esprit," *Le grand retour* (Istamboul 1953) 87-99.

64. Instruction to Odo, Cardinal of Tusculum, his legate to Cyprus, 1254: Mansi, XXII, 581-82; and cf. our study on Purgatory in *Le mystère de la mort et sa célébration* (*Lex orandi*, 12), (Paris 1951) 296-97.

65. The Decretal of Innocent IV, *Sub catholicae professione* of March 6, 1254, will alone furnish us with a great number: Mansi, XXIII, 578-82 (Potthast, II 15, 265).

66. Cf. P. Hammond, *The Waters of Marah: The Present State of the Greek Church* (London 1956) 24.

67. F. Braudel, *La Méditerranée et le monde méditerranéen à l'époque de Philippe II* (Paris 1949) 672.

68. Janin, "La prise de Constantinople (1453) et ses conséquences religieuses," *Nouv. Rev. théol.* 75 (1953) 511-19.

69. Pope Pius XII recalled these beneficent works in his Encyclical *Orientales omnes Ecclesias* of Dec. 23, 1945, for the anniversary of the Union of Brest: AAS, 1946, 45f.

70. Here we will reproduce only a few recent declarations that are rather representative: "Roman Catholicism has always been aggressive towards Orthodoxy. It has never recoiled before any effort to detach from the Orthodox faith entire populations whose political and cultural existence lacks a solid basis. . . ." Msgr. Anthony, Orthodox Archbishop of Finland, in the *Messager de l'Église* (St. Petersburg); reproduced in *Rev. internat. de théol.* 5 (1897) 111. What follows in the text rather frankly illustrates the word of Our Lord on the mote and the beam. N. Gloubokovski declared at the Conference of Stockholm in 1925 (Cf. *The Stockholm Conference 1925. The Official Report . . .* ed . by G. K. A. Bell, Oxford-London 1926, 654), "Proselytism of a purely pharisaical type has become a kind of disease of the new Romanism, and the conversion of the whole universe to the foot of the Roman Chair ha

become the bright vision and the sweet dream of the contemporary papacy. From these visions not one church is excepted, not one Christian con-- fession; they are all represented as the obligatory field for Catholic missionary practice, just as though they formed a purely heathen domain. Such among others is Anglicanism with all its ramifications. And as regards relations towards Orthodoxy everywhere, here the conduct of Romanism recalls the action of a rich and cunning landlord, who strives to get as much as possible of the goods of his sick and disheartened neighbor into his own hands, availing himself of every opportunity and of every possibility. I say this with great sorrow, but the facts cry out. In the East, the Mohammedan Crescent has been openly preferred to the Christian Cross. And in this direction the whole papal policy has been carried on which is now, for some reason, penetrated with Soviet sympathies, of course not for the sake of the tranquillity of Orthodoxy in Palestine. Against Orthodox Russia, moreover, there is divised, since the time of the unlucky Genoa Conference, some mysterious bond with the atheist Bolsheviks, and by consent of the latter, apostolic expeditions are fitted out, acquiring special purpose since the death of the Orthodox leader and common Christian martyr, His Holiness the Patriarch Tikhon." This enumeration of *gravamina* continues, but this will suffice to illustrate quite well the part played by subjectivity and short-sightedness in a reaction of this type. This attitude is a fact and it is quite typical. We hear the same sort of thing in the remarks of St. Zankow: "Dies ist das traurige Verhältnis zwischen den zwei ältesten und grössten christlichen Kirchen, der Römisch-Katholischen und der Orthodoxen: Zäher Eroberungsdrang einerseits, harte, stille Abwehr auf der andern Seite. . . ." *Die Orth. Kir. d. Ost. in ökumen. Sicht.* 60; cf. 26-27 and 54f, in which the Catholic Church is presented as always having sought unity by political means. All the same, we should take intelligent account of the situation and of the ideas of the time; cf. *infra*, ch. V, n. 32.

71. A frequent reproach; cf. Jugie, *Théol. dogm. christ. oriental. dissid.* IV, 407, n. 1; 420.

72. See also our Introduction to the French edition of Dvornik, *Le schisme de Photius: Histoire et légende, Unam Sanctam* 19, (Paris 1950) 12-15.

NOTES TO CHAPTER THREE

1. Cf. Jugie, *Le schisme byz.*, 39f. on the diversity of languages and reciprocal ignorance as one of the causes of the schism; Bardy, "La question
des langues dans l'Église ancienne," *Et. de théol. histor.* I (Paris 1948);
Michel, "Sprache und Schisma," *Festschrift der Freisinger Hochschule f.
Kard. Faulhaber zum 80. Geburtstag*, 37-69, which traces the process of
estrangement on the background of the ignorance of the respective languages from the time of Justinian. The point is not touched upon by
Greenslade, *Schism in the Early Church*. As a preparation for his book
or as an outgrowth of it, Bardy has written some very suggestive articles
summarizing the question, among others, "La latinisation de l'Église
d'Occident," *Irénikon* 14 (1937) 3-20, 113-30; "Orientalisme, occidenta-
lisme, catholicisme," *L'Année théolog.* (1947) 230-44.

2. Dölger, *Zeitschr. f. Kirchengesch.* (1937) 6-7.

3. Cf. Cardinal E. Tisserant, "Orient et Occident," *Rev. d'hist. eccles.*
67 (1952) 604-18; see also Michel, "Die griechischen Klostersiedlungen
zu Rom bis zur Mitte des 11. Jahrhunderts," *Ostkirchl. Studien* 1 (1952)
32-45; *id.* "Der kirchliche Wechselverkehr zwischen West und Ost vor
dem verschärften Schisma des Kerullarios," *ibid.* 145-73; H. Steinacker,
"Die römische Kirche und die griechischen Sprachkenntnisse des Früh-
mittelalters," *Mitteilg. d. Inst. f. Oesterr. Geschichtsforschg.* 62 (1954) 28-86,
treating the decline of a knowledge of Greek in the Fifth and Sixth Centuries; a recovery in the Seventh and Eighth.

4. St. Gregory Nazianzen says that the Latins do not distinguish Es-
sence and Person accurately, "because of the limitations of their language
and its poverty in words," quoted by Michel, *art. cit.* 46. In the discussions on the Procession of the Holy Spirit, the Greeks have often spoken
of the poverty of the language of the Latins, which made them, they
said, confuse "procession" with "mission"; cf. Jugie, *Le schisme byz.* 216,

227; Howard, *The Schism between the Oriental and Western Churches ...*, 103, on the response of the Orthodox Patriarchs to the English non-jurors in 1718. Cf. *infra*, n. 12.

5. The remarks of H. De Man, *Au delà du marxisme* (Paris 1929) 237 are very significant: "The mother-tongue is something else and more than the language of the mother, it is the veritable mother of the spiritual self. It is not merely the technical means of expressing an intellectual content of some kind; the content itself is determined, nay, in great part created, by it..." On the problem itself, see the indications given by Essertier, *Psychologie et Sociologie* (Paris 1927) 89f. and the reviews in *L'Année sociologique*, which pay a good deal of attention to this aspect of things; the special number of the *Journal de Psychologie normale et pathologique*, 30 (1933) on language. We should mention here the analyses of J. Guitton on the mind: cf. *La pensée moderne et le Catholicisme*, fasc. VI, "Le problème de Jésus," (Paris 1948) 191f. fasc. IX; "Développement des idées dans l'A. T. (Aix 1947) 85f; "Difficultés de croire," (Paris 1948) 76f.

6. The translation of "infallible" by a word which also signifies "impeccable" is evidently linked with the profound thought of the Eastern theology on infallibility which regards it as being connected with holiness and with the Holy Spirit; cf. Jugie, *Theol. dogm...* IV 465f; Gratieux, (*art. cit. infra*, n. 35) 359. The fact, however, makes it difficult for the Orthodox to perceive the true implications of papal infallibility which are, moreover, so often emphasized by us; it also leads them to say that we maintain the "impeccability" of the Pope; cf. Jugie, *op. cit.* 490f; Palmieri, *op. cit.* II 125, 127, 135; *et passim*. According to A. von Harnack, the Greeks do not have an equivalent word for *vicarius*: "Christus praesens-Vicarius Christi," ... . *SbBerlin*, 34 (1927) 415-446, n. 1.

7. This point is well known. At Florence, the discussion bore extensively on questions of vocabulary, on the equivalence of Greek and Latin terms. Pusey thought that the difficulty was a question of vocabulary. Cf. R. Gavin, *Some Aspects of Contemporary Greek Orthodox Thought* (Milwaukee 1923) 140 and 142. Among so many pages which deal with

this question, we should mention the very enlightening ones of Jugie, "St. Grégoire et la procession du Saint-Ésprit," *Échos d'Orient* 11 (1908) 321-31; 328-30.

8. See K. Holl, *Enthusiasmus und Bussgewalt* (Leipzig 1898) 417, n. 2. Scholarios employs for "satisfaction" the Greek word ἱκανοποίησις: DTC XIII 1, 1330.

9. Cf. J. Weisweiler, *Busse. Bedeutungsgeschichtliche Beiträge zur Kultur- und Geistesgeschichte* (Halle 1930) 228, 249. For our part, we believe that this is a very important point and marks the true difference between Eastern and Western thought. Cf. our study on Purgatory, *Le mystère de la mort....*

10. A propos of the Greeks being too subtle, the Roman apocrisiaries to the synod of Nicaea-Nymphaeum in 1234 complained of their "cavillationes": Mansi, XXIII, 280 C. Their perfidy was already noted by Cicero, quoted by Jugie, *Le schisme byz.* 28. Luitprand, Bishop of Cremona, took away this impression from Constantinople in 968; (Jugie, *ibid.* 158, n. 3.) The reproach was often formulated at the time of the Fourth Crusade; cf. Norden, cited *infra*, Ch. IV, n. 32.

11. Even as early as St. Gregory the Great, normally gentle, cf. *Ep. XX ad Mauritium Augustum* PL 77.746; Pope Vitalian in 668, cited by Jugie, *Le schisme byz.* 31; Pope John VIII, *Ep.* 108, ad Michaelem, regem Bulgarorum, PL 126.758C; and Pope Leo IX to Cerularius, PL 143. 748. For reasons justifying this approach, cf. Duchesne, *Churches Separated...* 73. See also Anselm of Havelberg, during the discussion of 1136 (*Dial.* III, 4 and 6: PL 188.1213C, 1215f.); III, 12 (col. 1226).

12. Cf. Michel, cited *supra*, n. 1; the constantly repeated reproach is clearly expressed in the polemic of Photius (cf. Jugie, *Le schisme byz.* 140) and of Cerularius (*ibid.* 216), and even in the irenic intervention of Peter of Antioch, 227. Nicholas I sharply took up these accusations in his response to Emperor Michael III: "We can only be astonished at seeing Your Majesty dare to mock the language of a Christian people as if it

were a barbarous and Scythian idiom. The barbarians and the Scythians live like mindless beasts, they ignore the true God and pray before stones and pieces of wood. ... You qualify Latin as barbarian because you do not understand it. But think, now, how ridiculous you become when you call yourself 'Roman Emperor' while not understanding anything of the Roman language..." PL 119.932. See also Palmieri, *op. cit.* II 53 and *supra*, n. 4.

13. Besides, Ch. 5, n. 22, *infra*, cf. H. I. Marrou, *History of Education in Antiquity*, (New York 1956) 340. Bréhier, *Monde byz.* III *La civilization byzantine* 420f., 456f.; R. Guilland, "La vie scolaire à Byzance," *Bull. Assoc. G. Budé* (March 1953) 63-83. Cf. *infra*, n. 37.

14. For *laicus* as equivalent to "illiterate" in the West, cf. our volume *Études conjointes pour une Théologie Laïcat*. For Byzantium, as well as the studies cited in n. 13 and *infra*, n. 32, and the well-known existence in the Empire of a body of well-educated laymen employed in the service of the State; cf. the fact that "Greek" sometimes signified "lettered, or cultivated man": E. Goldmann, "Graecus" = "Gebildet," *Mélanges Émile Boisacq*, (Brussels, 1937) 399-409.

15. C. Fleury, *Histoire ecclésiastique* (25 vols.) (Nîmes 1778-80) X 100.

16. Baumstark, *Grundgegensätze...* esp. 8-9, 11, 17-18, 33-43, 73. Cf. E. Goller, *Die Periodisierung der Kirchengeschichte und die epochale Stellung des Mittelalters zwischen dem christlichen Altertum und der Neuzeit* (Friburg 1919) 23; J. de Ghellinck, *L'essor de la Littérature latine au XIIᵉ siècle* (Paris–Brussels 1946) 12; de. Vries, *Der christliche Osten...* 21f.

17. Baumstark wrote before the most recent revival of Byzantine studies in the domain of religion and theology, or even art. One could not speak today, as in former times, of the static character of the East in its thought and art. The movement fostered by Palamas, which was really an anti-Scholastic reaction but has its own positive substance, surely cannot be called a phenomenon of "immobility" and old age. On the subject of art, see *L'Art sacré* (May-June 1953).

18. Cf. O. Rousseau. "La question des rites entre Grecs et Latins des premiers siècles au concile de Florence," *Irénikon*, 22 (1949) 233-69.

19. Bréhier, "Avant le schisme du XIᵉ siècle. Les relations normales entre Rome et les Églises d'Orient," *Docum. cathol.* 19 (1928) 387-404; citing J. Gay, *L'Italie méridionale et l'Empire byzantin*, 188.

20. Rousseau, *art. cit.* 267. The author spontaneously translates this "rite"; Hofmann, "Notae hist. de terminologia theologica Concilii Florentini," *Gregorianum* 20 (1939) 257-63, esp. 261-62.

21. This is a well-known point; it is particularly well expressed by Th. Kraline, "Paysans de Russie-blanche. Essai de psychologie religieuse," *Construire* 8 (1942) 92-119; esp. 110f.

22. Since we are not here treating the question *per se*, we will content ourselves with mentioning the profound pages of S. Boulgakov, *L'Orthodoxie* (Paris 1932) 194f. As testimony drawn from literature, see N. Gogol, *Méditations sur la divine Liturgie*. Introduction by Pierre Pascal (Paris 1952).

23. Cf. Kattenbusch, *Confessionskunde...* 118-19; the East tends to make the rite an absolute, the West a juridical interpretation, by which the rite becomes purely a means.

24. G. Florovski, "Problematical Aspects of Christian Reunion," (in Russian), *Put'*, n. 37, supplement: translated into French in *Irénikon* 11 (1934) 601; cf. Cl. Lialine, "De la méthode irénique," *Irénikon* 15 (1938) 239, note, and *Rev. Ét. byz.* 10 (1953) 157-58. The Orthodox are reproaching Uniatism, "the unija," for making the rite a *means* of obtaining a reunion which would in the long run be a pure and simple submission and therefore of not *truly respecting* the Oriental Church, intrinsically characterized by the rite.

25. "Considérations sur le schisme d'Israel dans la perspective des divisions chrétiennes," *Proche-Orient chrétien*, 1 (1951) 169-91.

26. To supplement these far too brief remarks, it would be well to read C. Korolevski, "L'Uniatisme," *Collection Irénikon* (1927), n. 5-6;

Lialine, *art. cit.* printed separately. Among the countless expressions of Orthodox reactions, one of the most characteristic is that of Msgr. Chrysostom Papadoupoulos, Orthodox Archbishop of Athens; cf. Hieromonius Pierre, "L'union de l'Orient avec Rome. Une controverse récente..." *Orientalia christ. period.* 18/1 (1930) 30f. and 54; cf. *Stoudion* 6 (Feb. 1929) 10f.

27. A. Wilmart, *Auteurs spirituels et textes dévots du moyen âge Latin* (Paris 1932) 59-60, 62, 506. Still other authorities might be mentioned.

28. These words compose the title of a chapter in *Corpus Mysticum*, H. de Lubac (Paris 1944); the entire book traces a history of the point under examination, which agrees with that of this passage.

29. See the works of Grabmann, Landgraf, Mandonnet, R. Martin, de Ghellinck, Chenu, and Gilson, of the centers in Saulchoir, Toronto, Ottawa, etc. Cf. also our article, "Théologie," in DTC. To give but one example: J.-P. Bonnes has edited and studied two sermons bearing upon the same subject, one by Geoffroy de Loroux (†1158), the others by Peter Comestor (†1178 ?-1179 ?). The former, still living in the atmosphere of the Church Fathers, considered the texts as a whole. The latter considered them through analysis and posed some questions: *quis, ubi, ad quid...?* J.-P. Bonnes, "Un des plus grands prédicateurs du xiie siècle, Geoffroy de Leroux, dit Geoffroy Babion," *Rev. bénédictine* 56 (1945-46) 174-215.

30. See Gratieux, A. S. *Khomiakov et le Mouvement slavophile* 2 vols. *Unam Sanctam* 5 and 6 (Paris 1939); cf. Kireevski, cited by E. Schultze, *Russische Denker* (Vienna 1950) 85-7 and cf. *in ra,* n. 35.

31. There is a very astute remark in this sense by Ph. de Regis, in his "Confession et direction dans l'Église orientale," *L'Église et le pécheur, Cahiers de la Vie spirituelle* 2nd ed. (Paris 1948) 132-150.

32. *Tertium est inscitia Graecorum. Periit enim apud eos pro magna parte scientia cum studio, et ideo non intelligunt quae dicuntur eis per rationes, sed adhaerent semper quibusdam conciliis, et quibusdam quae*

tradita sunt eis a praedecessoribus suis, sicut faciunt quidam haeretici idiotae, ad quos ratio nihil valet." *Opus tripart.* pars 2, c. 11; *ed.* Brown, 216. It is to be remarked that what Humbert notes is not in contradiction with what we said above on Byzantine culture: this culture was in the profane sciences, and theology was rather cut off from it, the Patriarchal school being something quite different from a University: cf. Bréhier, "Notes sur l'histoire de l'enseignement supérieur à Constantinople, "*Byzantion* 3 (1926) 84-85, and III of his *Monde byz.* 426f., 492f; Fuchs, "Die höheren Schulen von Konstantinopel im Mittelalter," *Byzantinisches Archiv* 8 (1926) 5; J. M. Hussey, *Church and Learning in the Byzantine Empire* (London 1937) 22-23, cited by C. Toumanoff, *Theol. Studies* (1946) 328.

33. In any case, not having accepted the knowledge of the Scholastics as having the status of religious knowledge. Such, of course, was the trend of the followers of Palamas. We are not unaware that in Byzantium there was during the Sixth Century and then in the Eleventh with Michael Psellos, something analogous to the Occidental dialectical movement of the Eleventh Century.

34. Cf. K. Pfleger, "Sinn und Sendung des neuorthodoxen Denkens," *Der christliche Osten* edd. v. J. Tyciak, G. Wunderle, P. Werhun (Ratisbon 1939) 259-74.

35. To the references given *supra* no. 30, add: Gratieux, "L'élément moral dans la théologie de Khomiakov," *Bessarione* (1910) 358-66; N. von Arseniev, "J. V. Kirejewskij und seine Lehre von der Erkenntnis der Wahrheit," *Kyrios* (1936) 233-44.

36. Cf. Dölger, "Zur Bedeutung von φιλόσοφος und φιλοσοφία in Byzantinischer Zeit," a survey reprinted in *Byzanz u. d. europ. Staatenw.* 193f.; cf. Vl. Valdenberg, "Sur le charactère général de la philosophie byzantine," *Rev. d'Hist. de la Philosophie* 3 (1929) 277-95, perhaps a little contrived; the best survey in French on the subject of Byzantine philosophy is that of B. Tatakis, which appeared as *Philosophie byzantine* in the 2nd supplementary section of *Histoire de la Philosophie* by Em. Bréhier, (Paris 1907) 217.

37. On this and many other points, J. Wilbois has been very perceptive in his *L'Avenir de l'Église russe* (Paris 1907) 217.

38. Jugie, "L'union facile avec les Orientaux?" *Unitas* (April 1949) 261-73; reprinted in the *Docum. cathol.* (Sept. 11) 1949, 1193-1206.

39. On the subject of Purgatory, cf. our study cited *supra*, *Le mystère de la mort...* 279-336, esp. 294f. Concerning the primacy, cf. Jugie, *Theol. dogm. or. diss.* IV 366f.

40. Quoted by St. Augustine, *De bapt.* 3, n. 5.

41. "La deification dans la tradition spirituelle de l'Orient," *Vie spirit.* Suppl. (May 1935), 91-108.

42. *Divided Christendom*, chs. I and IV. Vl. Lossky, *Essai sur la théologie mystique de l'Église d'Orient* (Paris 1944) 55 and 172: the disunion, according to Lossky, does not arise from differences of mentality or anthropological differences, but all the disagreements have their source in the one point of dogma, that which concerns the Procession of the Holy Ghost.

43. Thus J. B. Aufhauser writes: "Der letzte Grund der nahorientalisch-anatolischen Kirchenspaltung liegt nach meiner auf Grund langjähriger Studien wie vielfacher persönlicher Aussprachen mit nahöstlichen Kirchen-führern gewonnenen Überzeugung nicht so sehr in theologischen, als völkisch-kulturellen Unterschieden." "Die Theologie der getrennten Kirchen und die Frage der Wiederbegegnung," *Das Morgenländische Christentum* ed. P. Kruger and J. Tyciak, (Paderborn 1940) 79. We should merely add that the differences of mentality are in a very substantial way reflected in the theological structure itself.

44. We find in the "Great Catechism" of Philarete, which was, and perhaps still is, in use in Russia, the following question-and-answer: "Q.: What ideas and what recollections may we associate with the name of the Eastern Churches ? "A.: In Paradise, which was set in the East, was founded the first Church

of our first parents in innocence; in the East, too, after the Fall, was set the foundation of the Church of the redeemed, by the promise of the Savior. It was in the East, in the land of Judah, that Our Lord Jesus Christ, having consummated the work of our salvation, founded His own Church; it was from there that He spread the Church over the entire Universe. And until today, the Ecumenical Orthodox Catholic faith, confirmed by the seven Ecumenical Councils, is kept without change in its original purity by the ancient Churches of the East and in those Churches which are in agreement with them, as is by God's Grace, the Church of Russia." *The Doctrine of the Russian Church, being the Primer or Spelling Book, the Shorter and Longer Catechisms...* tr. by R. W. Blackmore (Aberdeen 1845) 82. As for the Patriarch Photius, the Latins arriving in Bulgaria came from *the darkness*, since they came from the West. (*Epist.* 4, 4, in ἐπιστολαί (ed. by J. N. Valetta, London 1864) 168. Analogous statements were made at the Council of Constantinople in 1054, quoted by Soloviev, *La Grande Controverse* 104.

45. *De la Méth. irén.* Offprint, 76.

46. It is an aspect of the *sobornost'* that must be kept in mind. Cf. E. von Ivanka "'Geisteskirche' und 'Gotträgervolk,' Zum Kirchenbegriff der Ostkirche," *Zeitschrif. kath. Theol.* 71 (1949) 347-54.

47. They are thus resumed by D. Stremoukhoff, *Vladimir Soloviev et son œuvre messianique* (Paris 1935) 203; with reference to the *Œuvres russes* V, 167-69: "Soloviev could therefore say that in the system of the Slavophiles, religion has no place, that their stylized Orthodoxy, their 'Orthodoxism' (*pravoslavnicanie*) is much more faith in the Russian people than in the Orthodox and Christian faith of that people. He was even to go further and declare that Orthodoxy is for the Slavophiles the true religion because the Russian people confess it, since it is 'an attribute of the Russian nationality.'"

48. "God sums up in Himself a whole people. When the peoples begin to have common gods, it is already a sign of their decline. Each people, in order to remain a separate ethnic group, should have its own God."

And cf. H. Kohn, *Prophets and Peoples, Studies in Nineteenth Century Nationalism*, (New York 1946) ch. 5.

49. See the analysis made by Palmieri, *Theol. dogm. orth.* 11, 156f.

50. N. Oehmen, "*Le 'lieu théologique' du Schisme et le travail pour l'Union*," *Irénikon*, 17 (1945) 26-50.

NOTES TO CHAPTER FOUR

1. Epist. *Quantum presbyterorum* to Acacius, Jan. 9, 476 PL 58. 42.
Denzinger, *Enchiridion Symbolorum* no. 159; St. Basil in his *Epist.* XC,
PG 32.473; in 372 and especially St. Gregory of Nazianzen, *Carmen de
vita sua*, PG 37.1068, in 382: "In nature, there is only one sun, but there
are two Romes, one of which illumines the West, the other the East";
however, ancient Rome, "Unites all the Occident by a true teaching, which
is just, since she presides over the whole and guards the universal and
divine harmony." We say, "if not from the beginnings": there has been
from the beginning an East and a West. St. Irenaeus, wanting to express
the catholicity of the Church, enumerates three churches of the Occident
(Germania, Iberia, Gaul) and three churches of the Orient (East—Antioch, etc.—Egypt, Libya) and those of the middle world (Rome?); but
he primarily stresses that the apostolic tradition is the same in all these
churches, which are as one sole house. PG 7.552. Cf. St. Augustine,
Contra Jul. 1.13, P. 44.649A: "utriusque partis terrarum fides."

2. Bardy, "Le sens de l'unité dans l'Église et les controverses du Vᵉ
siècle," *L'Année théolog.* 9 (1948) 169. Very impressive is the following
text of H. Lietzmann: "So it came about that the synod which had been
called as representing the whole Empire, fell asunder from the first, breaking into two halves, each of which condemned and deposed the leader of
the other. Then each party returned home, the question now being which
of them would be able to carry out its will. Schism had become a fact.
For the first time in the history of the Church, East and West separated
from each other by formal decision. It was not merely differences in
church politics that found expression in the present division; there were
also differences both in theological thought beneath the ambiguous formulae, as well as in many aspects of religious feeling, as between Eastern
and Western Christianity. A straight line runs from Sardica to the final
separation in A.D. 1054." *From Constantine to Julian,* trl. by Bertram Lee
Woolf (New York 1950) 206.

3. See Jugie, *Le schisme byz.* 60.

4. Lietzmann, *op. cit.* 205.

5. On the subject as a whole, see Cavallera, *Le schisme d'Antioche* (*IVe–Ve siècles*) (Paris 1905); Schwartz, "Zur Kirchengeschichte des vierten Jahrhunderts," *Zeitschr. f. Neutestamentliches Wissen.* 34 (1935) 129-213; Devreesse, *Le Patriarcat d'Antioch...* (Paris 1945).

6. Cf. the remark of St. Ambrose in his *Ep. XIV* to Theodosius: "Dolori erat inter Orientales atque Occidentales interrupta sacra communionis esse consortia." PL 16.954. See Palanque, *S. Ambroise et l'Empire romain ...* (Paris 1933) 96f. 505. It is not certain that *Orientales* in this text has the restricted meaning of applying to the diocese of the Orient.

7. Cavallera, *op. cit.* 299.

8. The favor the Eastern Fathers showed towards human liberty derives from their sociological background. Bardy, *op. cit.* n. 2, *supra*, 167, writes: "[... the Pelagian affair] throws into relief the depth of the abyss which had insensibly been made between the Greek Church and the Latin Church. Not only did the two Churches not speak the same language, but they did not concern themselves with the same questions. The Orientals, who are mystics, were concerned with the way man should achieve the vision of God and, better still, achieve divinization. The Westerners, who are moralists and jurists, were, on the contrary, concerned with the question of how man should render his account to God...." Note also remarks of the same tenor made, beginning with the liturgy, by Baumstark, "Grundgegensätze...," 54f.

9. See the monumental work, *Das Konzil von Chalkedon. Geschichte und Gegenwart*, Grillmeier and Bacht, I, the survey by Ch. Moeller, "Le chalcédonisme et le néochalcédonisme de 451 jusqu'à la fin du VIe siècle," II; the article by Hoffmann, *ibid*, "Der Kampf der Päpste um Konzil und Dogma von Chalkedon, von Leo dem Grossen bis Hormisdas, 451–519."

10. In the Roman liturgy, from the beginning, the stress is rather more on the element of instruction than on the mystical. Baumstark, *loc. cit.*

11. "Quomodo incrementum influxus orientalis in Imperio byzantino s. VII-IX dissensionem inter Ecclesiam Romanam et Orientalem promoverit?" *Acta Con. Pragensis pro studiis oriental.* (Olomouc 1930) 159-72; cf. 166-171.

12. *Supra* ch. I, n. 40. and Ch. Diehl, *Histoire de l'Empire byzantin* (Paris 1920) 59f.

13. Cf. Michel *supra*, ch. I, n. 3, 532.

14. See the text and the studies made of them in P. Baron, *Une théologie orthodoxe, A. S. Khomiakov* ... (1940) 153f.; also *L'Église latine et le protestantisme au point de vue de l'Église d'Orient* (Lausanne and Vevey 1872) 33f. 86 ("moral fratricide"); *Birkbeck and the Russian Church*... collected and edited by A. Riley, (London 1917) 343.

15. See the numerous historical treatments of the question, the articles on the *Filioque*; Howard, *op. cit.* 22-30. The difficulties raised by the Carolingian councils were the cause of a certain delay in counting the Council of 787 among the Ecumenical Councils; cf. Dvornik, *Les légendes de Constantin et de Méthode vues de Byzance* (Prague 1933) 306f.

16. Besides Hergenröther, see: Duchesne, *The Churches Separated*...; Bréhier, *Le schisme oriental du XIᵉ siècle* (Paris 1899); *id. Cambridge Mediaeval History* IV 246-273, ch. IX: *The Greek Church; its Relations with the West up to 1054* (Cambridge, 1923); J. Pargoire, *L'Église byzantine de 527 a 847* (Paris, 3rd. ed. 1923) gives the facts but touches only occasionally on the problems as a whole; Ivanka, "Orient et Occident: Une contribution au problème du schisme," *Irénikon* 9 (1932) 409-21; Congar, *Div. Christendom.*, 3-14; A. Hamilton Thompson, *The Division between East and West* (brochure, reprinted in *Union of Christendom*, ed. by K. Mackenzie, London, 1938, 109-32) 455f. Jugie, *Le schisme byz.* 232, on Cerularius: "The true cause of the schism was the indomitable determination of the Byzantine Patriarch to maintain his full autonomy vis-a-vis the Roman pontiff"; Michel "*Kampf...*" D. *Konzil von Chalkedon.* II 491-562. See also V. Monachino, *infra* n. 20; Herman, *infra* n. 27.

17. See Palmieri, *Theol. dogm. orth.* II 139.

18. See Heiler, *Altkirchliche Autonomie* . . . on Milan, 96f.; on Aquilleia, 108; on Aix-la-Chapelle, cf. Jordan, *Nouv. Rev. hist. droit* (1921) 364. The theme: *Translatio studii* E. Gilson, "L'Humanisme Médiéval," *Les Idées et les Lettres* (Paris 1932) 184-85.

19. Council of Constantinople, 381, Canon 3 (Mansi, III 557f.) See W. Bright, *The Canons of the First Four General Councils* . . . with notes (Oxford 1892) 106-11. As we have already seen and as we shall see later on, the year 381 is a notable date in the process of estrangement. If Damasus did not reject the Canon, at least the text of the Council of 382 (cf. *infra*, n. 35) is implicitly a criticism of it; cf. Jugie, *Le schisme byz.* 87-88.

20. Council of Chalcedon, 451, Canon 28, (Mansi VII 357f). Bright, *op. cit.* 219-233; Jugie, *Le schisme byz.* 12, whose translation we follow in part. The studies made of Canon 28 are numerous and recent: J. Chapman, *Bishop Gore and the Roman Catholic Claims* (London 1905) 86f. Batiffol, *Le Siège apostolique* (Paris 1924) VIII; Jalland, *The Life and Times of St. Leo the Great* (London 1941) 303f.; Schwartz, "Der 6. Nicänische Kanon auf der Synode von Chalkedon," *SbBerlin* 27 (1930); A. Wuyts, "Le 28ᵉ canon de Chalcédoine et le fondement du Primat romain," *Orient. christ. period.* 17 (1951) 265-82; Monachino, "Genesi storica del Canone 28° di Calcedonia" *et* "Il Canone 28° e S. Leone *Magno*," *Gregorianum* 33 (1952) 261-91 and 331-65; Th. O. Martin, "The Twenty-Eighth Canon of Chalcedon. A Background Note, "*Das Konzil von Chalkedon, Gesch. u. Gegenwart* II 433-58.

21. *Epist. CV* to the Empress Pulcheria (22 May, 452) PL 54.995.

22. "Alia tamen ratio est rerum saecularium, alia divinarum; praeter illam petram quam Dominus in fundamento posuit, stabilis erit nulla constructio." *Epist. CIV* to the Emperor Marcian (22 May 452) PL 54.995. Cf. Gelasius I to the Bishops of Dardania (1st Feb. 495) PL 59.71-72.

23. Cf. Jugie, "Le plus ancien recueil canonique slave et la primauté du pape," *Bessarione* 34 (1918) 47-55; A. D'Alès, "Le 28ᵉ canon de Chal-

cédoine dans la tradition de l'Église serbe," *Rech. Sc. relig.* 12, (1922) 87-89;
M. d'Herbigny, *Theologica de Ecclesia* II § 293. That the *Nomocanon* was
not drawn up by St. Methodius himself (cf. *Échos d'Orient* 1936, 503)
does not lessen the force of the fact here signalized.

24. That is to say, according to the scheme of the three principle Sees,
(Rome, Alexandria, Antioch) linked with the Apostle Peter: cf. the
history of this theory in Michel, *Der Kampf...*, 500-524. It is to be regretted
that several times in history Rome actually linked her best-founded claims
to historical fictions, e. g. when she claimed to be the origin of all the
Western Churches. Even St. Leo's interpretation of Canon 6 of Nicaea
is not entirely invulnerable to discussion.

25. Cardinal Humbert was to call Cerularius "Bishop of the Imperial
city." Michel, *Der Kampf...* 518-19.

26. The first bishop of Constantinople to have adopted this title seems
to have been Acacius, thus giving rise to the protestation of Pope Felix II
(Jalland, *The Church and the Papacy* 315; Michel, *Der Kampf...* 497).
Before him, the title had been given without great significance other
than honorary, to Dioscoros of Alexandria (449) by St. Leo. As is well
known, when John IV, The Faster, bestowed upon himself this title in
586, Pope Pelagius and St. Gregory the Great protested with vehemence
and insistence. St. Gregory saw in it a title of pride, regarded it as a
profane and ambitious and monopolizing title, by means of which the
reality of their episcopate was implicitly refused to the other bishops.
Cf. S. Vailhé, "Le titre de Patriarche oecuménique avant St. Grégoire le
Grand," and "S. Grégoire le Grand et le titre de Patriarche oecuménique,"
Echos d'Orient 11 (1908)65-69 and 161-71. After John The Faster and
his successor Cyriacus, the title became current in Constantinople, but it
was only Michael Cerularius who introduced it into the patriarchal seal,
where it afterwards remained; Laurent, "Le titre de patriarche oecuménique et la signature patriarcale. Recherches de diplomatique et de si-
gillographie byzantines," *Rev. hist. du Sud-Est européen* (1946) and "Le
titre de patriarche oecuménique et Michel Cérulaire. A propos de deux
de ses sceaux inédits," *Miscellanea Giovanni Mercati* III 373-386 (Vatican
1946). On the meaning of "oecumenical" cf. *supra*, ch. I, n. 6.

27. Besides those studies cited n. 142, cf. Herman, "Chalkedon und die Ausgestaltung des Konstantinopolischen Primats," *Das Konzil von Chalkedon* II 459–90.

28. Cf. Mirbt, *Quellen zur Gesch. d. Papsttums* n. 204; C. Kirch, *Enchir. Fontium Hist. ecclesiast. ant.* n. 1035-1036.

29. Canon 36: Mansi, XI 959; Kirch, *op. cit.* n. 1096.

30. Dvornik, "La lutte entre Byzance et Rome à propos de l'Illyricum au IXe siècle," *Mélanges Charles Diehl* (Paris 1930) 61–80; *Les légendes de Constantin et de Méthode vues de Byzance* 248–83; R. Honig, *Beiträge zur Entwicklung des Kirchenrechtes* (Göttingen 1954) 30f.

31. We give a few references only, less to prove these assertions which will be evident to anyone versed in the texts, than to clarify what we wish to say. We allude, for example, to ecclesiological studies such as those of the contemporary Greek theologians so well summarized by Gavin, *Some Aspects...* 237f; the collection of testimony on the Church gathered by J. A. Douglas, *The Relations of the Anglican Churches with the Eastern Orthodox* (London 1921) App. I, 115–135, or again the many studies by Russian Orthodox theologians, of which we will list the main ones. Macarius (Boulgakov) *Théologie dogmatique orthodoxe* (French translation Paris 1860) II 219f.; Msgr. Serge, Bishop of Yamburg and Rector of the Ecclesiastical Academy of St. Petersburg, "Qu'est-ce qui nous sépare des anciens catholiques?" Fr. transl. *Rev. internat. de Théol.* 12 (1904) 175–188; Serge Boulgakov, speech made at the Ecumenical Conference of Faith and Order, Lausanne, 12 August 1927, *Foi et Const. Actes Officiels...* (Paris 1928). 296–303; Florovsky, "Le Corps du Christ vivant," *La Sainte Église universelle. Confrontation oecuménique (Cahier théol. de l'Actualité protestante)*, (Neuchâtel–Paris 1948) 9–57. Shades of differences are to be detected here and there, and even some slight emendations. But on the whole, studies such as these display a profound identity of dogmatic opinion on the mystery of the Church. For the position of the priesthood and of the people, cf. Kattenbusch, *Lehrb. d. vergl. Confessionskd.* I 346f., and the two volumes of our *Jalons....*

32. Zankov, *Die Orthod. Kirche des Ostens in ökumen. Sicht*, 52-54.

33. For this reason, after citing above the texts assembled by Canon Douglas in his Appendix I (The Church, its Composition and Infallibility...) as evidences of our accord on the mystery of the Church, we now cite those he groups in Appendix II of the same work, 163-73: "The Oecumenical Church and the Autocephalous Churches", as evidences of our opposition: at this point what is involved are the constitution, the regime, the policy of the Church.

34. We recommend the collection of texts (accompanied by a brief and very objective *status quaestionis*) *Documents Illustrating Papal Authority A. D. 96-454* (ed. and intr. by Giles, London 1952): the author stops with St. Leo but, with the Russian Orthodox historian Bolotov, or with another Anglican historian, one may say that the Petrine and Roman ideology, formulated by St. Leo in order to prevent Constantinople from isolating herself within a closed ecclesiastical autonomy, was the one taken up by the Vatican Council: B. J. Kidd, *The Roman Primacy to A.D. 461* (London 1936) 153. In addition, there are the classic surveys by Duchesne, *The Churches Separated...*; J. Chapman, *Studies on the Early Papacy* (London 1928); Batiffol, *Le catholicisme des origines à S. Léon* 4 vls. (Paris 1909-1924); *Catholicisme et Papauté, Les difficultés anglicanes et russes* (Paris 1925) *Cathedra Petri. Et. d'hist. anc. de l'Église* (Paris 1938); S. H. Scott, *The Eastern Churches and the Papacy* (London 1928); Jalland, cf. *supra*, ch. I n. 13; Jugie, *Le schisme byz.* "Où se trouve le christianisme intégral?" (Paris 1947). Monographs on this subject abound.

35. Of special importance is the decree taken up again in the *Gelasianum* Mirbt, n. 191, which in reality is of the Roman synod of 382 (Damasus) and corresponds to the Council of Constantinople of 381 (*supra* n. 19); it contains a very strong affirmation of the universal primacy of Rome.

36. Cf. Mirbt, n. 139, 145-155; H. Gebhardt, *Die Bedeutung Innocenz für die Entwicklung der päpstlichen Gewalt* (Leipzig 1901).

37. For St. Leo, cf. Batiffol, Kidd, Jalland (cited *supra*) and the numerous works on the Primacy of Chalcedon. For Gelasius, cf. various works of Schwartz, Kissling, H. Koch, without forgetting Vol. II of Caspar.

38. Mirbt, n. 195. Cf. W. Haacke, *Die Glaubensformel des Papstes Hormisdas im Acacianischen Schisma* (Rome 1929); J. San Martin, "La 'Prima sedes' del Papa Hormisdas (514-523)," *Rev. española de Teol.* I (1940-41) 767-812.

39. A good statement on the primacy at the turn of the Fourth to Fifth Centuries is to be found in Bardy, *Hist. de l'Église*, (Fliche et Martin 4) 241f. See Jugie, *Le schisme byz.* 57f.: a good number of these facts and statements are, however, to be placed in the perspective of a simple canonical *prima sedes*.

40. Cf. S. Salaville, "La primauté de S. Pierre et du pape d'après S. Théodore Studite," *Échos d'Or.* 17 (1914) 23-42; Jugie, *Le schisme byz.* 94-96. For St. Nicephorus, see Apologeticus Major, c. 25 PL 100.597.

41. Palmieri, *Theol. dogm. orth.* II cites only Simeon of Thessalonica († 1429) 57: PL 145.100. Jugie, *Théol. dogm. christ. oriental, diss.* IV 366f. cites a rather large number of authorities; cf. "De B. Petri Ap. Romanique Pontif. Primatu a theologis byzantinis etiam post schisma consummatum assertio...," *Angelicum* 6 (1929) 47-66. But some of them speak of the primacy in a vague and indeterminate way. Besides, a great difference may be noted between the texts by Orientals and the texts subscribed to but not drawn up by them, those of the councils of union, for instance, among others the profession of faith of Uroch III of Serbia addressed to Pope John XXII, p. 373. Thus, even in the documents of union may be noted the permanence of what is the cause and actual substance of the schism, the existence of two different canonico-ecclesiological points of view. The testimony of the historians should also be noted: cf. for example, in Jugie, *op. cit.* 402f., those of A. P. Lebedev, V. V. Bolotov and N. Suvurov.

42. Cf. Batiffol, "L'Ecclésiologie de S. Basile," *Échos d'Orient*, 21 (1922) 18f.

43. Jugie, *Le schisme byz.* 62f. does not quote any text and with good reason. A. Moulard, *St. Jean Chrysostome* (Paris 1941) 116, recognizes this absence and states well John's concept of the status of Rome. Much

has been written on this subject. Card. N. Marini, *Il primato di S. Pietro et dei suoi successori in S. Giovanni Crisostomo* 2nd ed. (Rome 1922); J. Hadzega, *Acta III. Conv. Velehradensis* (Prague 1912) (but what is dealt with here is the primacy of Peter, while the whole question bears on that of *the pope* and the connection this question has with that of Peter...); Jugie, "S. Jean Chrysostome et la primauté du pape," *ibid.* 193–202.

44. The texts cited by Jugie, *Le schisme byz.* 83–84, speak of *Peter.*

45. *Cathedra Petri. Et. d'Hist. anc. de l'Église,* (*Unam Sanctam* 4, Paris 1938) 75–76. This idea that Rome and the East do not give the same content to the concept of primacy, emerges from the (Anglican) book by H. E. Symonds, *The Church Universal and the See of Rome...* (London 1939). Moreover, the question should not be too lightly dismissed. Some Roman documents accepted in the East expressly argue that the authority exercised by the Bishop of Rome derives from the authority of the Apostle Peter, exercised by the Bishop of Rome. For example, the letter of Pope Julius to the Eusebians: Athanasius, *Apol.* 35, and that it resides in the Roman See-Formula of Hormisdas; cf. the study by Haacke cited *supra* n. 38. Of course, not forgetting Sardica.... Occasionally but rarely, one even runs across the idea that Peter himself is incarnated in the Bishop of Rome; Theodore Abu-Qarra (Syria, † 867?) Ignatius of Constantinople, at Nicaea in 867: cf. Jugie, *Le schisme byz.* 96–97 and 90.

46. "Normal relations between Rome and the churches of the East before the schism of the Eleventh Century," *The Constructive Quarterly* (Dec. 1916) 645–73: French text in *Docum. cathol.* 19 (1928) 387–404.

47. *Cathedra Petri,...* 41–59; special application to the East, 199–214. The account given by Bardy, cited *supra* n. 29 well illustrates the idea which is a simple statement of facts. The same may be said of the book by Heiler, cited *supra* n. 18.

48. Batiffol, *Siège apostolique...,* 577f; Kidd, *Rom. Primacy* 152–53.

49. Jugie, "Interventions de S. Léon le Grand dans les affaires intérieures des Églises orientales," *Miscellanea P. Paschini* (Rome 1948) I 77–94.

50. Michel, "Der Kampf...," *Das Konzil von Chalkedon* II 544-54.

51. The earlier studies of Dvornik, outlined for a wider public in several articles, "Le patriarche Photius, père du schisme ou apôtre de l'union?" *La Vie intell.* (Dec. 1945) 16-28; "East and West: The Photian Schism. A Restatement of Facts," *The Month.* 179 (1943) 257-70, have been taken up as a whole again in the work cited *infra* n. 76. See also Jugie, "Photius et la primauté de S. Pierre et du pape," *Bessarione* 35 and 36 (1919 and 1920) 121-30 and 16-76; *Le schisme byz.*, 90-93. M. Gordillo, "Photius et Primatus Romanus," *Oriental. christ. period.* 6 (1940) 6-39; (the polemic: "To those who claim the Primacy for the See of Rome," is not by Photius; it dates from the Thirteenth Century. But this study by Gordillo has been critizised by Jugie, "L'opuscule contre la primauté romaine attribué à Photius," *Ét. de Critique et d'hist. relig.*, *Publ. de la Fac. cath. de Théol. de Lyon*, 2 (Lyon 1948) 43-60.

52. Cf. Dvornik, art. mentioned *supra* n. 11, 76.

53. Here are the last lines of his fine study, which opens such interesting vistas: "The schism which has shattered our souls was not wanted by the faithful but was imposed upon them by the politicians. After centuries of fearful crises, the Churches of the West and the East had managed to establish a regime of mutual harmony which had not attained perfection but could endure and be improved. A whole series of usages, traditions, practices, assured between them normal and peaceful relations; on the greater portion of the terrain where their interests might be in opposition, they had reached compromises; the autonomy of the Churches of the East was not incompatible with the dogmatic and disciplinary authority of the Holy See; and finally, the daily interchanges between their congregations could become the best token of their unity. Had the question remained in the domain of religion, the accord would have become definitive. Unfortunately, the ambitions of the Patriarch Michael Cerularius began to clash with the resistance of the legates sent by Leo IX, and there was no longer room for anything but the schism."

54. The reply of the Orthodox to the idea outlined above, that the primacy had been affirmed and exercised for centuries without causing the East to interrupt communion, is generally that communion was pre-

cisely interrupted by Nicholas I, who first made a radical theological theory of the primacy. Cf. Jugie, *Theol. dogm.*... IV 407. This reply is in sum, not historically valid, but contains a seed of truth we will try to take into consideration in the following pages.

55. Cf. N. Milasch, *Das Kirchenrecht der morgenländischen Kirche*, 2 ed. Mostar 1905) 93-95; as to the exact position of Photius in regard to this subject, cf. Dvornik, *The Photian Schism*, 92.

56. On the debate with Carthage (Apiarius), cf. Chapman, *Stud. on the Early Papacy* 184f. H. E. Feine, *Kirchliche Rechtsgeschichte* I (Weimar 1950) 81, 97f. For the epoch of St. Leo, cf. Jalland, *The Ch. and the Papacy* 312.

57. Aside from what has been said above, cf. ch. II, n. 19, 20, see the original and penetrating remarks of Kattenbusch, *Lehrb. d. vergl. Confessionskunde* 331-35.

58. Again, a remark of Kattenbusch, 361. The collegial idea is deeply rooted, moreover, in Eastern social history: cf. "La personne et la liberté humaines dans l'anthropologie orientale," *Recherches et Débats*, (May 1952) 99-111.

59. Cf. the account by Bardy in the *Hist. de l'Église* (Fliche et Martin 4) 184, and n. 4.

60. Session III (13 Oct. 451): Mansi, VI 1047: "Unde sanctissimus et beatissimus archiepiscopus magnae et senioris Romae, Leo, per nos et per praesentem sanctam synodum, una cum ter beatissimo et omni laude digno beato Petro apostolo qui est petra et crepido catholicae ecclesiae et rectae fidei fundamentum, nudavit eum Dioscorum tam episcopatus dignitate quam etiam et ab omni sacerdotali alienavit ministerio."

61. Epist. CIII, PL 54.992. I am indebted for this juxtaposition to W. Schneemelcher, "Chalkedon, 451-1951," *Evangelische Theologie* (1951) 241-45.

62. Cf. Jugie, *Le schisme byz.* 19; Bréhier, *Monde byz.* II 489-90. On the origins of the permanent synod see a rather unfriendly notice by

H. Leclercq, *Hist. des conciles* II/1, 519, n. 1. On Chalcedon, cf. Mansi, VII 92f. For the ulterior development of the institutions: B. Stephanidis, "Die geschichtliche Entwicklung der Synoden des Patriarchats von Konstantinopel," *Zeitschr. f. Kirchengesch.* 55 (1936) 127-57.

63. Bréhier, *Hist. de l'Église* (Fliche et Martin 4) 535f. Milasch, *op. cit. supra*, ch. III, n. 55.

64. There is a good exposition in Symonds, *The Church Universal and the See of Rome* 209f; and cf. Jugie, *Le schisme byz.* 26-27, 45.

65. Pichler, *Gesch. d. kirchl. Trennung zw. Orient u. Occident* I 87f. And see, *infra*, Photius and Cerularius. Mirbt gives as title to n. 224, wherein are quoted a good number of these canons: "Abgrenzung der Kirche des Ostens gegen das Abendland in Recht, Gottesdienst u. Sitte." It would naturally be unfair to say that Rome has never in any way recognized the legitimate differences of discipline between the East and herself. The pronouncements and the facts in this matter are numerous, but they do not pertain to our present theme.

66. This important dispute went on from 905 to 923; cf. Amann, *Hist. de l'Église* (Fliche et Martin 7) 116-25, especially this last page.

67. Cf. P. Fournier and G. Le Bras, *Histoire des collections canoniques en Occident* I (Paris 1931) 79, and also most particularly, W. M. Plöchl, *Geschichte des Kirchenrechts* II (Vienna–Munich 1953) 256f. Plöchl names the year 692 as a crucial point in his "Periodisierung."

68. See the texts of *Collectio antiariana Parisina* n. 17 and 26, CSEL, LXV, 59 and 65: "Verum nos iterum illos atque iterum rogabamus, ne firma solidaque concuterent, ne subverterent legem nec jura divina turbarent, ne cuncta confunderent atque traditionem Ecclesiae ne quidem in modica parte frustrarent..."; "Nec hoc propter bonum quoque justitiae inquirunt, non enim ecclesiis consulunt, qui leges juraque divina (ac) ceterorum decreta dissolvere perconantur, propterea hanc novitatem moliebantur inducere, quam horret vetus consuetudo Ecclesiae, at, in concilio Orientales episcopi quidquid forte statuissent, ab episcopis Occidentalibus

refricaretur, similiter et, quidquid Occidentalium partium episcopi, ab Orientalibus solveretur, etc..." Cf. Greenslade, *Schism in the Early Ch.* 156.

69. Cf. Jugie, *Le schisme byz.* 57-58.

70. *Id., op. cit.* 63-64.

71. For example, the letter of Gelasius, *ad Dardanos*, Feb. 1, 495 (Jaffé, 664); double text in PL 59, 61f., or Thiel I, 382f. A decisive passage, taken up again in the Occidental canonical collections is, for example, Gratian, c. 17 C. IX q. 3 (Friedberg, I 611).

72. We owe this remark, as well as those concerning the False Decretals, to Hartmann, *Der Primat des römischen Bischofs bei Pseudo-Isidor* (Stuttgart 1930) 28.

73. This affair has been traced by Heiler, *Altkirchliche Autonomie...* (see our review in *Rev. des Sc. philos. et théol.* 1947, 276f.)

74. For Nicholas I, cf. J. Haller, *Nikolaus I. und Pseudo-Isidor* (Stuttgart 1936) (not very favorable to Rome). Cf. *supra* n. 54. Concerning the False Decretals, we need not repeat what is today universally admitted, that they were not the acts of Rome but of Frankish clerics, seeking to ensure to the Church her independence in regard to the secular powers. But they contributed to the increasing of papal power and the ideology expressing that power. Cf. Fleury, *Hist. ecclesiast.* 4th "Discours" at the beginning of Vol. XVI, and Haller, *op. cit.* Hartmann, *op. cit.* 28, has shown that the Pseudo-Isidore has the popes using the same imperative terms with the Eastern bishops that they employed in their metropolitan or Western competence. The pontifical texts of the False Decretals treat the bishops of the whole world as suffragans of the Pope, with the obligation of conformity, not only in the faith, but in discipline and usages. On the point under consideration, this is the contribution of the False Decretals. It is important to note that the decisive affirmations of Nicholas I on his authority in regard to the councils, are to be found in the documents anterior to the "reception" of the False Decretals by Rome; cf. Gordillo, *Compendium Theol. Orient.* 2nd ed. (Rome 1939) 80.

75. One of the best accounts of the development of the exercise of pontifical power is that of V. Martin, art. *Pape* in the DTC XI/2, 1877f. Cf. Jugie, "Où se trouve...," 35-6, 208f.

76. See. V. Grumel, "Y eut-il un second schisme de Photius?" *Rev. des Sc. philos. et théol.* 12 (1933) 432-57; Jugie, "Origine de la controverse sur l'addition du *Filioque* au Symbole," *ibid.* 18 (1939) 369-85, and *Le schisme byz.* 101f. Amann, various articles (among others, the articles *Jean VIII* and *Photius* in DTC, and portions of *Hist. de l'Église* (Fliche et Martin 7). Dvornik, numerous studies resumed in *The Photian Schism, History and Legend* (Cambridge 1948.)

77. Jugie, *Le schisme byz.* 141, remarks: "In Rome they seemed to forget the true situation of the Byzantine Church in relation to the Western Church on the canonical plane. In his letters on the Photius affair, it is not rare to find Pope St. Nicholas and his secretary, Anastasius Bibliothecarius, calling upon the Decretals of the popes to show the illegalities of which Photius was guilty. Now, the Byzantine Church totally ignores this source of the canon law. Even for the sources which are common, there are many divergencies in the details. This is so, for example, in the canons of Nicaea and Sardica, some of which had already fallen more or less into disuse in the Byzantine Church..." Ostrogorsky, *Gesch. d. byz. Staates* 2nd ed. 189, has well, if briefly, noted the difference of canonico-ecclesiological concepts existing between the Greeks and the Roman legates at the Council of 869-70.

78. Photius wrote to Nicholas I: "The authentic Canons should be kept by all, but principally by those whom Providence has called to govern others; and among the latter, those who have received a share of the primacy should outshine all others in faithfully observing them." PG 102.616; cited in Jugie, *op. cit.* 92-3. At the Synod of St. Sophia in 879-880, Photius had it decreed that each Church should remain faithful to her particular customs: "Each see observes certain ancient customs, which have been transmitted by tradition, and one should not enter into dispute and litigation on this subject. The Roman Church conforms to her particular usages, and that is proper. On her side, the Church of Con-

stantinople..." (Jugie, *op. cit.* 143). This formula is unassailable if it is not made to imply that each Church is fully autonomous. By this reasoning, too, Photius justified the canonically debatable circumstances of his promotion to the patriarchate.

79. Cf. Dvornik, *The Photian Schism* 145-50.

80. Cf. Jugie, *op. cit.* 139f.

81. Cf. the encyclical addressed by him to the Oriental Patriarchs after the Synod of 867; Jugie, *op. cit.* 113.

82. Jugie, *op. cit.* 232-33.

83. See Michel, "Bestand eine Trennung der griechischen und römischen Kirche schon vor Kerullarios?" *Hist. Jahrb.* 42-(1922) 1-11; *Humbert und Kerullarios* (Paderborn, 1924 and 1933) I 20f. and II 22f. Jugie, *op. cit.* 170, 221; Ostrogorsky, *Gesch. d. byz. Staates* 267; Amann, *Hist. de l'Église* (Fliche et Martin 7) 126: "The separation of the two Churches of Rome and Constantinople has not yet been consummated in fact as it has been in the literature." But Amann does not admit the rupture which Michel, for example, ascribes to Sergius II; Herman, "Le cause storiche della separazione della Chiesa Greca secondo le piu recenti ricerche," *La Scuola cattolica* (1940) 12-14; Grumel, "Les préliminaires du schisme de Michel Cérulaire ou la question romaine avant 1054," *Rev. des Ét. byz.* (1953) 5-23.

84. Michel, 10-11; Jugie, 168. Bréhier, II 487.

85. Jugie, *Le schisme byz.* 230.

86. Cf. Mirbt, n. 269; French translation in Jugie, *op. cit.* 206f. On Humbert and Cerularius, Michel, *Humb. u. Kerull.* 2 vls. reviewed in *Byzantion* 2 (1926) 615-19, by M. Viller, and 8, 1933, 321-26 by Jugie; *id.* "Lateinische Aktenstücke und -sammlungen zum griechischen Schisma, (1053-1054)" *Hist. Jahrb.* 60 (1940) 46-64 (he calls Humbert "Sturmvogel der gregorianischen Reform", "der heissblütige Stürmer").

87. Cf. Herman, "I Legati inviati da Leone IX nel 1054 a Constantinopoli erano autorizzati a scomunicare il patriarca Michele Cerulario?" *Oriental. christ. period.* 8 (1942) 209–18; we share the opinion of others (cf. *Irénikon* 1954, 153) that the mandate of the legates was still valid.

88. Amann, *Hist. de l'Église* (Fliche et Martin 7) 139f; Ostrogorsky, *Gesch. d. byz. Staates, 2nd ed.* (who notes that it was not cesaropapism which caused the break.)

89. Laurent, *Miscell. Mercati* III 373–96.

90. Cf. Jugie, *op. cit* 212f. 216, 231f.

91. Cf. Michel, *art. cit,* in following note, 74.

92. On the ecclesiological ideas of Humbert and their connection with those of the Gregorian reform, cf. Michel, "Die folgenschweren Ideen des Kardinals Humbert und ihr Einfluss auf Gregor VII," *Studi Gregoriani* I (Rome 1947) 65–92; Ullmann, "Cardinal Humbert and the Ecclesia Romana," *ibid.* (1952) II 111–27; Michel, *Die Sentenzen des Kardinals Humbert, das erste Rechtsbuch der päpstlichen Reform* (Leipzig 1943). For a hypothesis on the origin of the *Dictatus Papae* (March 1075): J. Gauss, "Die Dictatus-Thesen Gregors VII als Unionsforderungen, *Zeitschr. d. Savigni-Stiftung, Kanon. Abt.* 29 (1940) 1–115.

93. Cf. V. Buffon, *Chiesa di Cristo e Chiesa Romana nelle lettere di Fra Paolo Sarpi* (Louvain 1941) 62.

94. This is the opinion of Michel, *op. cit.* 77, n. 3. and of Every, Introd. n. 1, who received the approbation of Bréhier, *Rev. historique,* 199 (1948). 263–64; K. Jordan, "Zur päpstlichen Finanzgeschichte im 11. und 12. Jahrhundert," *Quellen u. Forschg. aus ital. Archiven,* 25 (1933–34) 61–104 and "Die päpstliche Verwaltung im Zeitalter Gregor VII," *Studi Gregoriani* I (Rome 1947) 111–35.

95. Cf. Norden, *Das Papsttum und Byzanz* (Berlin 1903) 97f. and 203f. Nicetas of Nicomedia, in his dispute of 1136 with Anselm of Havelberg,

reproached the Roman Church for wishing to decide everything, alone, by her authority: Anselm of Havelberg, *Dialog.* III 8, PL 188.1219.

96. At the synod at Nicaea–Nymphaeum in 1234, the *Basileus* said: "The schism has lasted for close to three hundred years." (Cf. Mansi, XXIII, 297, D.) He was therefore counting it from the year 1054.

NOTES TO CHAPTER FIVE

1. See for example Jugie, *Le schisme byz.* 252-53, 258 (Twelfth and Thirteenth Centuries). Cf. for the Orthodox viewpoint, L. Gafton (in Rumanian), "The Aggravation of the Schism, following the Attempts at Union made in the period from the 11th to the 15th centuries," *Orthodoxia* (Bucharest) 8 (1956) 397-410.

2. As a sampling· of such differences (and not a comprehensive list), we may mention the expression "transsubstantiation" (first employed about 1130); the theology of indulgences (first attested concessions in 1016, then at the Council of Clermont, 1095) and, in a general way, the insistence on the aspects of penal satisfaction (St. Anselm), with consequences as to our way of understanding Purgatory (cf. our study cited *supra*, ch. III, n. 39); the development of the theology of papal power and the tendency to exercise it in sense of *plenitudo potestatis*, the tendency towards centralization; the restriction of canonizations to the pope, etc.

3. Cf. Algermissen, *Konfessionskunde...* 577.

4. Such attempts were that of John the Scot, a movement which ended with the condemnation of 1241. Cf. M.-D. Chenu, "Le dernier avatar de la théologie orientale en Occident au XIIIᵉ siècle:" *Mélange Aug. Pelser* (Louvain 1947) 159f. H. F. Dondaine, "Hugues de Saint-Cher et la condemnation du 1241," *Rev. des. Sc. phil. et théol.* (1947) 170-74, and *Rech. Théol. anc. et med.* 19 (1952) 60f. Mendoza on the Eucharist in the Sixteenth Century; cf. *Rev. des. Sc. phil. et théol.* (1950) 401-2. Here we may add, in recent times, the theology of the liturgical mysteries of Dom Odo Casel, *ibid.* 60 and the "new theology", linked to the current rediscovery of the Orient as to the interpretation of biblical sources. There were, indeed, some fortunate successes or at least, half-successes. Apart from the influence of Denis the Areopagite (who was not followed in all his

oriental themes), there were the Cistercians (St. Bernard and William of St. Thierry), Nicholas of Cusa, Petavius and Scheeben.

5. See Epist. *CCXI* PL 214.771: "If the Patriarch invited by us comes (to the general Council...) we will receive him benevolently and joyfully as a beloved brother and one of the principal members of our Church. On other matters, by the authority of the Apostolic See and with the approbation of the Holy Council, with his advice and the advice of the other brethren, we will enact what should be enacted." Hofmann, "L'idée du concile oecuménique comme moyen d'union dans les tractations entre Rome et Byzance," *Unitas* 3 (July 1950) 25-33.

6. Cf. R. Scholz, "Eine Geschichte und Kirchenverfassung vom Jahre 1406," *Papsttum und Kaisertum...* (*Festg. P. Kehr*), (Munich 1926) 595-621; cf. 607, n. 3.

7. Cf. Aubert, *Le pontificat....* 402-26.

8. Already in 1169-1177, and therefore before the conquest by the Latins, the Patriarch Michael Anchialus declared: "Let the Saracen be my Lord in outward things, and let not the Italian run with me in the things of the soul, for I do not become of one mind with the first, if I do obey him, but if I accept harmony in faith with the second, I shall have deserted my God, whom he, in embracing me, will drive away." Every, *Byzantine Patriarchate* 184-85. At the Council of Florence, Dositheus, Bishop of Monemvasia (Morea) said: ἐγὼ βούλομαι ἀποθανεῖν, ἢ λατινίσαι ποτὲ (Mansi, XXXI/A 885C). Cf. Gloubokovski cited *supra*, ch. II, n. 70. Preferring the turban to the tiara, the Greeks defended Constantinople without enthusiasm: Diehl, *Hist. de l'Empire byzantin* 199-209.

9. We are alluding to the distinction established by Möhler between "Gegensatz" and "Widerspruch." Journet translates: contrast and contrary.

10. *Concilium Tridentinum Diariorum, actorum, epistularum, tractatuum nova collectio.* Ed. S. Ehses, Societas Goerresiana (Freiburg i/B. 1901-1951) V/2, 870 (*Articuli haereticorum...* n. 7). The theologians of Wittenberg were later to find the Byzantine theologians equally ill-disposed. One

of them, Zygomalas, gave them the following response at the beginning of the Eighteenth Century: "Etsi Christus ipse de coelo descenderet, dicens Spiritum Sanctum a Patre et Filio procedere, tamen Graecos id non esse credituros." (Gavin, *Some Aspects...* 141, n. 1.)

11. We should like to quote here some truly irenic texts; see the one of Peter of Antioch, PG 120.796f; Jugie, *Schisme Byz.* 225f, and that of Theophylactus, PG 126.221f; Jugie, 243.

12. P. Tournier, *Médecine de la personne* 5th. edit. (Neuchâtel-Paris 1941) 211f.

13. *Opus tripartitum* pars 2, c. 14; (Edit. Brown) II, 218.

14. *Ibid.* 214.

15. The Roman conception of the unity of the Church, he said, could be rather well shown by the analogy of a plate with the letter *P* on it which is unbreakable because when broken the fragment with *P* on it is the plate. F. Claude Kempson, *The Church in Modern England* (New York 1908) 202, cited in C. Smyth, *The Appeal of Rome; its Strength and its Weakness* n. d. (1945 or 1946) 9.

16. *Epist. LXVI*, (Edit. Hartel, CSEL) VIII 723.

17. See *Acts* 2.41-2, 47; cf. 9.26.

18. The faithful "those who were with the twelve," *Mark* 8.45 and *Luke* 24.33. The Apostles "those who were with Peter," *Mark* 1.36; *Luke* 8.45 and cp. 5.1-11, and for the sense, *Luke*, 22.31-2.

19. See Congar, *Jalons...* 638-39.

20. Humbert of Romans, *op. cit.* pars 2, ch. 6f. (Brown, II 211f.) has, in this respect, some particularly interesting formulas. The popes have often joined to the institution by Our Lord, the mention of "patrum decreta" (the Councils), and the imperial recognition (*Donatio Constantini*), etc.

21. To such effect that, as Leo XIII remarked (*infra*, n. 29), we may illustrate many of our doctrines by Oriental testimonies. Here we will restrict ourselves to quoting some words of Pius XI: "Eucharistiae sacramentum percolamus, pignus causamque praecipuam unitatis, mysterium illud fidei, cujus amorem studiosamque consuetudinem quotquot Slavi Orientales in ipso a Romana Ecclesia discessu conservarunt... Ex quo tandem sperare licebit... Alterum unitatis reconciliandae vinculum cum Orientalibus Slavis in eorum singulari studio erga magnam Dei Matrem Virginem ac pietate continetur, eos ab haereticis compluribus sejungens, nobisque efficiens propriores..." *Encycl. Ecclesiam Dei* 12 Nov. 1933 for the third centenary of St. Josaphat: *Acta Ap. Sedis* 15 (1923) 581. And finally see our "Note sur les mots 'Église,' 'Confession,' et 'Communion,'" *Irénikon* 23 (1950) 3–36.

22. Cf. Bréhier, *art. cit. supra, Docum. cath.* col 400f. This excellent Christian historian who in his considerable work has given perhaps the most exact picture of things, is fond of stressing the elements of non-opposition.

23. See *supra*. Ch. IV, n. 50 and 52. Thirty years before Cerularius, Pope John XXI had not been intractable: Jalland, *The Church and the Papacy* 399; Innocent III (cf. Tillmann, *Papst Innocenz III*, 216f.) and Innocent IV (cf. *infra*, n. 37) while conceiving the union to be more than anything, a submission to the authority of the Roman See, still did not utterly reject the idea of a Uniate Church statute that, in principle, would be respectful of the Oriental rite. At Florence, Rome agreed to leave undiscussed the points already defined as dogma in the West: Hofmann, *art. cit.* 97, n. 3.

24. Jugie, *Le schisme byz.* passim, has given quite a few references on this subject.

25. If the reconstruction of events attempted by Grumel is exact, Rome seems to have taken the initiative towards a reconciliation in the year 1062: "Le premier contact de Rome avec l'Orient après le schisme de Michel Cerulaire," *Bull. Littér. ecclésiast.* 43 (1952) 21–29.

26. We have in mind essentially the conversations held (1) between the Orthodox and the Old-Catholics at Bonn in 1874 and 1875; (2) between the Anglicans and the Orthodox in the Eighteenth, Nineteenth and Twentieth Centuries,—the journey of P. Puller in Russia in 1912; the report of the mixed commission published in 1932—; (3) between the Orthodox and the Catholics, cf. *Russie et Chrétienté*, n. 3-4. We hope to indicate elsewhere the documentation and the results of these exchanges. Evidently to be pointed out among the causes of a better comprehension is the publication, by Th. De Regnon, of his remarkable *Études de théologie positive sur la Ste. Trinité* 4 vols. (Paris 1892–1898).

27. This was the decisive matter, if not for Photius himself (Jugie says "no" in the article cited *supra* n. 76, and in *Le schisme byz.* 143-46; Grumel says "yes" in *Rev. des Ét. byz.* 5 [1947] 218-234), then at least for Cerularius, perhaps even for the Irenicals, Peter of Antioch and Theophylactus (Palmieri, *Theol. dogm. orth.* II 30-32); again in the attempt at reconciliation in the year 1062, and, fundamentally, until the Council of Florence (Palmieri, *supra* and 82), at which, moreover, the question of the primacy, perhaps slightly camouflaged, seems not to have caused great difficulty. At the synod of Nicaea-Nymphaeum in 1234 and at Lyons, the Greeks raised only two difficulties: regarding the *Filioque* and the Azymes. Among the causes of discord, Humbert of Romans gives very little place to questions of doctrine, and mentions only the *Filioque*, (*op. cit.* 2, c. 18: Brown, II 222).

28. Some of the Orthodox do not blame the *Filioque* in itself but only its unilateral insertion into the Creed; thus, for example, A. S. Khomiakov, writing to W. Palmer: cf. *Russia and the English Church*, ed. Birkbeck, 60f.; or Msgr. Gerasino Messara, Greek-Arab Metropolitan of Beyrouth in his letter of 1910; cf. *Échos d'Orient* 14 (1911) 48-51. Today, the greater number of the Orthodox say that the *Filioque* is not a heresy or even a dogmatic error but an admissible theological opinion, a "theologoumenon." Thus, in a very positive way, Soloviev; cf. his "Questions" in d'Herbigny *Vladimir Soloviev, Russian Newman* tr. A. M. Buchanan (London 1918) 166. Similarly, as early as the Twelfth Century, Nicetas of Nicodemia; cf. Van Lee, *Les idées d'Anselme de Havelberg sur le développement des dogmes*

(Tongerloo 1938) 10 and n. 26; and again, in contemporary times, Bolotov, Florovsky, Boulgakov (cf. Hadžega, "Der heutige orthodoxe Standpunkt in der Filioque-Frage," *Theol. und Glaube* 34, [1942] 324-330) which gives the references.) Many consider that the *Filioque*, correctly understood, should not be an obstacle to reunion; thus Lossky, *Irénikon* (1938) n. 24, Eulogius and Svetlov, *Rev. des Ét. byz.* (1953) 162. Cassien and several professors of the Institut St. Serge, *Russie et Chrétienté*, (1950) n. 3-4. One could also bring other testimonies to bear. In touching lightly upon the question, Gavin, *Some Aspects...* 134-143, does not mention such clear and positive statements emanating from Greek theologians as the sampling of testimonies we have just given, which come almost entirely from Russian theologians.

29. Thus, for example, Msgr. Elias Meniate, Bishop of Zarissa, *La pierre d'achoppement* Germ. transl. Vienna, (1787) cited by De Maistre, *Du Pape*, 417; the Procurator of the Holy Synod, C. Pobedonoscev; Prince G. Troubetskoy (cited by Th. Spacil, *Oriental. christ. period.* 2 (1924) 95, n. 1; Boulgakov, *Put'* (May 1929) 47-48. To these let us add the following text of Leo XIII: "Si pauca excipias, sic cetera consentimus, ut in ipsis catholici nominis vindiciis non raro ex doctrina, ex more, ex ritibus, quibus Orientales utuntur, testimonia atque argumenta promamus. Praecipuum dissidii caput, de Romani Pontificis primatu..." Letter *Prae-clara gratulationis*, June 20, 1894: *Acta* 14 (1895) 199; ed. B. Presse, *Lettres et Actes de Léon XIII* V 86-88.

30. *Cathedra Petri...* 79. Cf. our preface to *Photius* by Dvornik, 17-21.

31. The list of these would be impressive. Very many studies exist; we will cite only, besides Norden in the following note, and studies mentioned *infra*, n. 35., the rapid survey of Smit, *Roma e l'Oriente cristiano, L'azione dei Papi per l'unità della Chiesa* (Rome 1944).

32. Cf. Hergenröther, *Neue Studien über die Trennung der morgenländi-schen und abendländischen Kirche* (Würzburg 1865) 169f; Norden, *Das Papsttum und Byzanz. Die Trennung der beiden Mächte und ihre Wiederver-einigung bis zum Untergang des byzantinischen Reiches (1453)* (Berlin 1903). See also Jugie, *Le schisme byz.* 197, 252; Fliche, "Le problème oriental au

second concile œcuménique de Lyon, 1274," *Mélanges de Jerphanion, Orient. christ. period.* 13 (1947) 475-85;ʻ Viller, "La question de l'Union des Églises entre Grecs et Latins depuis le concile de Lyon jusqu'à celui de Florence, 1274-1438," *Rev. d'Hist. ecclés.* 17 (1921) 260-305, 515-32; 18 (1922), 20-60. Cf. *supra* ch. II, n. 70.

33. P. R. Regamey in *La Maison-Dieu* 26 (1951/2) 159.

34. See G. Goyau, *L'Église libre dans l'Europe libre* (Paris 1920).

35. See the very interesting but incomplete collection in A. d'Avril, *Documents relatifs aux Églises de l'Orient considérées dans leur rapports avec le Saint-Siège de Rome* (Paris 1862); again the list of documents, complete within the indicated limits, with quotations from important passages, in J. Schweigl, "De unitate ecclesiae orientalis et occidentalis restituenda, documentis S. Sedis ultimi saeculi (1848-1938) illustrata," *Periodica de re morali, canonica, liturgica* 28 (1939) 209-33. See also A. Korenec, *S. Sedes Apostolica et disciplinae graeco-catholicorum agitur de Calendario* (Vienna 1916). For documents on the union of Brest, sometimes unjustly criticized by the Orthodox, for it was based on respect for the rites and customs, cf. Hofmann, "Wiedervereinigung der Ruthenen mit Rom," *Oriental. Christ. period.* 3 (1924) 125-72. And, for an overall view of the attitude of the Holy See and its development, cf. Aubert, *Le Saint-Siège et l'union des Églises. [Chrétienté nouvelle]* (Brussels 1947).

36. It is clear in Aubert, *op. cit.* 83; cf. Herman, "Églises orientales, catholiques et dissidentes," *Unitas* 2 (July 1949) 17-27.

37. For Photius, cf. *supra* ch. IV, n. 57; for the Bulgarians, *ibid.* n. 58. In the dealings carried out under Innocent IV (who, for his part, sacrificed the Latin Empire of the Orient), the Greeks accepted the following conditions: recognition of the papal primacy, oath of obedience of the Greek clergy, obedience to the decisions of the pope in so far as they be not contrary to the canons of the Councils, the Roman curia as jurisdiction of appeal, the right of the pope to preside over Councils, and to vote first at these; cf. Norden, *Das Papsttum...* 369. Complete this with Hofmann, "Patriarch von Nikaia Manuel II an Papst Innozenz IV," *Oriental. christ. period.* 16

(1953) 59-70. A church dignitary as authoritative as Msgr. G. Calavassy, declared that the Oriental Churches, while remaining autocephalous, could nevertheless find their place in Catholic unity. Cf. *Irénikon* (1955) 173.

38. *Op. cit.* 145.

39. Since they state an exact fact and express very significantly a true feeling, we will here quote these lines that end the splendid collection of the *Procès-verbaux du Premier Congrès de Théologie orthodoxe à Athènes*; 29 Nov.-6 Dec. 1936 (Athens 1939) 506: "We have noted with particular joy that in reporting the First Congress of Orthodox Theology in Athens, both the official organ of the Vatican and the daily and periodical Catholic press have commented upon it with interest and at length... It is true that no least excuse for displeasure was given the Catholic Church during the sessions of the Congress. On the contrary, the divergent points, as they came up for discussion, were handled respectfully and with tact. The correctness and dignity of the articles that appeared in the Catholic press incontestably produced an excellent impression in Orthodox circles. This will perhaps serve on later occasions as a first important step toward bringing about a good attitude and a Christian and holy understanding between the two Churches."

40. Douglas, *The Relations of the Anglican Churches...* 95.